Steve shines the light of truth on the corruption currently crippling Corporate America. In the era of Sarbanes-Oxley, as corporate leaders and board members are looking for the proper tools to equip their organizations, I pray they utilize the biblical blueprint that Steve lays out for a return to ethical corporate governance and a restoration of faith in the American corporate system.

—KEITH E. KRZEWSKI, COO
BAKER & MCKENZIE, SAN DIEGO, CA

As a businessman I realize the importance of integrity and sense of responsibility, which begin with the leaders and involve every employee. We are becoming increasingly aware of the massive cost of corporate fraud, mismanagement, and misrepresentation to the American economy. It can no longer be ignored. Steve Austin with Mary Steelman has written a book that seeks no less than to inspire a Reformation in Corporate America.

—JAMES P. GILLS, MD, CEO
ST. LUKE'S CATARACT AND LASER INSTITUTE
TARPON SPRINGS, FL

I am extremely excited about the whole book, the way it has been written, and especially the timely message it has to business leaders in America. America's leaders must align their ethics with time-proven biblical principles, or our leaders will continue to fail and further corrupt our nation and its businesses. I endorse this book and recommend it be read by every person in business.

—RAY BERRYMAN, CHAIRMAN AND CEO
BERRYMAN AND HENIGAR, ORLANDO, FL

After Enron and others, now we all know the devastating impact of somehow thinking that business insulates us from the values upon which lasting civilizations have been established. This book provides a clear analysis that explores the major issues and lays out the resulting problems and effects of compromising our values in the workplace. What a reminder of the value of keeping a biblical perspective in our daily lives—and that the best way to avoid sliding down the slippery slope is to stay off of it!

—STEVE DEAL, PRESIDENT AND CEO
INDYME ELECTRONICS, SAN DIEGO, CA

I found the contents to be challenging opportunities and at the same time a great encouragement to continue pursuit of the highest degree of integrity.

America is long overdue to accept the challenge that this book presents.

—Dan Ford, Chairman
Eagle Plastics and Rubber of TN, Inc.

Steve Austin provides a clarion call to a reformation of business practices based on biblical principles. He seeks to bring order out of chaos through a sound and inspiring application of godly wisdom.

—Vince Siciliano, CEO, First Pacific Bank
San Diego, CA

Winning organizations in the twenty-first century will be those with leaders who have the capacity for continuously modeling ethical practices and behaviors. By advancing tried and true spiritual principles with direct application to our lives, Steve and Mary present solid solutions to the challenges associated with greed and shortcuts found today with ever-increasing regularity within Corporate America.

—Doyle Young, Coauthor, *The Everchanging Organization*
Cofounder and CEO
The EverChange Institute, San Diego, CA

New laws and regulations offer little hope of preventing future frauds and scandals. They are good as far as they go, but they do not (and, in my judgment, cannot) go far enough. By shining a light on the real issue—matters of character and integrity, matters of the heart—this book provides genuine hope for reducing the likelihood of future abuses like the ones we've seen in recent years.

—Jack E. Wilkerson Jr., Dean
Wayne Calloway School of Business and Accountancy
Wake Forest University
Winston-Salem, NC

Whether you are a shareholder of a corporation, a member of its board of directors, or part of senior management, it is critical to understand and insist upon the right set of standards of integrity and ethics for Corporate America in light of the dramatic fallout in business ethics over the last four years. This book makes an unassailably compelling case for the standards that are the key to success and provides a great historical perspective of the basis for those standards. It belongs in the boardroom of every corporation.

—Michael Changaris, Attorney
Procopio, San Diego, CA

RISE OF THE NEW ETHICS CLASS

Life After Enron: Not Business As Usual

RISE OF THE NEW ETHICS CLASS

STEPHEN G. AUSTIN with MARY STEELMAN

Charisma
HOUSE
A STRANG COMPANY

Most STRANG COMMUNICATIONS/CHARISMA HOUSE/SILOAM products are available at special quantity discounts for bulk purchase for sales promotions, premiums, fund-raising, and educational needs. For details, write Strang Communications/ Charisma House/Siloam, 600 Rinehart Road, Lake Mary, Florida 32746, or telephone (407) 333–0600.

RISE OF THE NEW ETHICS CLASS by Stephen G. Austin with Mary Steelman
Published by Charisma House
A Strang Company
600 Rinehart Road
Lake Mary, Florida 32746
www.charismahouse.com

Unless otherwise noted, all Scripture quotations are from the New King James Version of the Bible. Copyright © 1979, 1980, 1982 by Thomas Nelson, Inc., publishers. Used by permission.

Scripture quotations marked KJV are from the King James Version of the Bible.

Scripture quotations marked NIV are from the Holy Bible, New International Version. Copyright © 1973, 1978, 1984, International Bible Society. Used by permission.

Scripture quotations marked NLT are from the Holy Bible, New Living Translation, copyright © 1996. Used by permission of Tyndale House Publishers, Inc., Wheaton, IL 60189. All rights reserved.

Scripture quotations marked THE MESSAGE are from *The Message: The Bible in Contemporary English*, copyright © 1993, 1994, 1995, 1996, 2000, 2001, 2002. Used by permission of NavPress Publishing Group.

Cover design by Mark Labbe
Interior design by Terry Clifton

Library of Congress Cataloging-in-Publication Data

Austin, Steve, 1952-
Rise of the new ethics class / Steve Austin.
    p. cm.
Includes bibliographical references.
ISBN 1-59185-450-4 (hardcover)
  1. Business ethics. 2. Christian ethics. 3. Wealth--Moral and ethical aspects.
  4. Corporate culture. 5. Executives. I. Title.
HF5387.A85 2004
241'.644--dc22   2003024678

04 05 06 07 — 87654321
Printed in the United States of America

Dedication (Stephen G. Austin)

To my wonderful wife, Gail, who for years has tolerated this personality-Type-A/multitasking CPA who cares deeply for her and our three wonderful children.

~~~

To Krista Gail, Stephanie Faith, and Sarah Elizabeth, who will carry the banner of integrity and Christian ethics into their lives and help change the world.

Dedication (Mary A. Steelman)

To Ed, who gave me daily support and encouragement for this project. Thank you for believing in me.

~~~

To my son, Matt, whose integrity and strength of character have given me insight into my own.

Acknowledgments

This book is the result of the efforts of a team of wonderful professionals who have joined in the vision of Reformation for Corporate America. I would like to thank the following:

- Ms. Lois Babcock and Dr. James P. Gills of St. Luke's Cataract and Laser Institute, Tarpon Springs, Florida, for their kind efforts to get this project started.

- Mr. Frank Mustachio for all his good help with the development of our book Web site.

- Tom and Joanne Cook, without whose help and encouragement of Mary Steelman, this project might not have occurred.

- Pastor Barry Minkow, who inspired me to complete this text and stay focused on a biblical message to today's problems in Corporate America.

- The many fine Christians at Charisma House and Strang Communications Company who believed in this author and wanted a strong biblical answer to the crisis in the business world.

- Reverend William Shishko, Ms. Edith Markham, Dr. Karen Hanson, and Erin Hattenburg for their insightful comments and perspectives on the message of this book.

- Last but not least, my executive assistant, Diane Lopez, the world's greatest New York Yankees fan, who tirelessly completed the book's manuscript preparation and managed all the meetings and details to make this book possible.

Contents

Foreword

There is something to be said of God's perfect timing. In approximately 473 B.C., Mordecai brought this realization home when he showed Esther how she had been raised up to become part of God's sovereign plan to deliver Israel from certain doom. Esther, as queen of Persia, faced a moral dilemma, and yet she chose to keep her integrity intact. Facing tremendous odds to do what was right, her cousin Mordecai encouraged her with these words: "Who knows whether you have come to the kingdom for such a time as this?" (Esther 4:14).

As in the story of Esther, deceit and lack of ethics have always portrayed a moral dilemma since the beginning of time. God elevated Esther to a place of authority to save her people. In like manner, I believe God has raised up Steve Austin to address the ethical decay of Corporate America.

In the first half of 2003, the FBI was opening three to five new cases of fraud involving $100 million or more each month.[1]

The crisis at major corporations such as Enron, WorldCom, Global Crossing, Peregrine, and Homestore due to fraud and accounting errors cost the stockholders and taxpayers more than $1 trillion. That figure exceeds the $600 billion loss that resulted from the 9/11 tragedy.[2] It is not my intention to affix a dollar amount to the precious loss of life we experienced on September 11, 2001. Life is priceless. I am, however, comparing the economic loss and its impact on our economy. The CEOs of these failed companies did tremendous damage to the lives of their employees and the shareholders who believed enough in them to invest their life savings.

The story is told of a pastor who had announced to his congregation that he would be leaving his church. After the service, as he was greeting the people on their way out, a visibly distraught woman approached him in tears. Feeling an inner sense of gratitude that this woman was so upset about him leaving, the pastor attempted to console her. "Don't worry, ma'am. I'm sure that the next pastor will be far better than me," he said humbly. Taking little comfort in his words and without missing a beat, she said, "That's what they told me when the last pastor left before you came—but they just keep getting worse!"

Just because things "keep getting worse" in our society, we can no longer dismiss them as the aberrant misgivings of a few. For this reason, *Rise of the New Ethics Class* is long overdue. Steve Austin has taken the current corporate climate of pragmatism and greed, aligned it with Scripture, and came up with practical applications that can be implemented in every public boardroom across the country. His approach of proactive fraud prevention, which begins with the "Tone at the Top," is cutting-edge thinking that will result in an ethical Reformation for Corporate America. Bookshelves of bookstores are strewn with books on this subject, but they merely address the symptoms (unethical business practices) and fail to address the root of the problem—greed and deceit. This book has come into His kingdom "for such a time as this."

—BARRY MINKOW, SENIOR PASTOR
COMMUNITY BIBLE CHURCH, SAN DIEGO, CA

Wealth from get-rich-quick schemes quickly
disappears; wealth from hard work grows.
—Proverbs 13:11, nlt

CHAPTER 1

Chaos and Confusion

Betsy Atkins was the newest member on the Board of Directors of HealthSouth. As most new directors do, she approached her new role as chair of the special litigation committee with passion. But she was completely unaware of the underlying problems. Then those underlying problems surfaced suddenly and unexpectedly. Nevertheless, she stayed the course and approached the task with objectivity. During her short stay, she kept a journal of the events that transpired.

> I was elected a director of HealthSouth on March 7, 2003, and spent much of the first couple of weeks thinking through the things I needed to do in my role as chair of [the board's] special litigation committee. Then came March 19, and everything seemed to fall apart. I got several early-morning phone calls from the other board members, telling me that FBI agents were showing up in large numbers at various HealthSouth facilities around the country.[1]

Betsy was a central figure at HealthSouth as investigators probed deeper into the company's financial status. She chaired many meetings and gathered the information necessary to try and stabilize the company. Less than a month after accepting the position, she resigned.

Todd Thomson, Citigroup's CFO, established the "Tone at the

Top" from the very beginning. In an interview with *CFO* magazine, Thomson said, "I want a culture of integrity in the finance organization. That happens only if I'm viewed as having personal integrity."[2] The plight in Corporate America is real.

There is a mounting crisis in the United States business community as never before. This crisis is the fruit of decades of dishonesty and greed. This book has one objective: to clearly illustrate that our business climate is infected with a cancer that, if not treated soon, will reduce us to a meager nation.

This book is a call for Reformation in Corporate America. It is a call for the reversal of an attitude that we can somehow "con" our economy into prosperity. The denial factor in the business world is huge. The resistance from top-level executives to take the "right course of action" is monumental. Today's media are screaming every day that we have a moral collapse in American and international business (as evidenced by the alleged scandal at Parmalat).

The cure for what we face today is very simple: ethics and integrity in business are matters of the heart. The only way to bring about a real change is to change the hearts of men and women.

This book is designed to offer a bridge from the crisis that engulfs us to a future that envisions integrity and substantive prosperity. This is a bridge between two vast lands: today's morass of financial fraud, greed, and SEC investigations to a landscape of relative calm and ethical standards that are derived from the Authority that created us.

How Do We Start the Reformation?

After thirty years of public accounting, I have made my living by asking tough questions and looking for accounting errors and misstatements. Over the last several months we have witnessed an avalanche of business failures in many of the most "sophisticated" corporate environments in America. The root cause of what we are witnessing today is man's innate propensity to look for shortcuts or some way "around the rules." In effect, we are trading our long-term future for short-term greed.

Thousands of employees of Enron, WorldCom, Global Crossing, and scores of other fallen corporate empires and businesses have lost their jobs from 2000–2003. The shakeup in Corporate America changed the financial landscape of accounting practices forever.

The tragedy of September 11, 2001 shook the United States' financial and economic foundations to the core. Economic predictions of financial recovery suggest that the economy would take years to recover. The trauma of September 11, 2001 had barely settled when the restatement of the financial results of an energy company based in Houston, Texas, sent shock waves throughout the business community. Enron's disclosure of accounting errors and material misstatements of their previously reported financial results set off widespread life-threatening trauma throughout the U.S. business infrastructure, the aftershocks of which continue today in a domino effect.

Undoubtedly, the economic cost of September 11, 2001 was monumental in terms of loss of life, property damage, and disruption of our economy. But the fall of Enron and other large U.S. companies that followed wreaked a different havoc on us. These companies' dealings have left us with an underlying distrust of the U.S. accounting systems and shattered our sense of trust and business ethics. The 9/11 tragedy also devastated the tangible—lives, buildings, and our sense of security. The financial scandals of Wall Street devastated the tangible *and* the intangible—our faith in accounting practices and our confidence in each other.

Even more shocking, this crisis has occurred without the evil machinations of terrorists from foreign nations. Rather, we have done it to ourselves.

Analysis of a Crisis

Since the fall of 2001, I have been asked to speak at dozens of conferences and business meetings. The most common questions that I am asked to address are:

1. Can you put into perspective what has happened to American business since 2001?

2. Can you help us understand what we need to do to correct these problems?

3. How do we keep this from occurring again?

I will address in greater detail these same three points throughout this book. The vision of this book is to ignite a "Reformation in Corporate America," whereby faith-based principles and biblical guidelines replace America's current weak ethical foundation. I'm not asking you to necessarily agree with me; but I do ask that you seriously consider these insights as potential fundamental reasons behind today's crisis and possible solutions for the future.

The following pages set forth a ten-point analysis of the prevailing reasons behind today's crisis and helps bring this crisis into perspective.

FAILURE IN BUSINESS ETHICS	
Problem	**Effect**
Management integrity	Nondisclosure of all facts/ unwarranted wealth
Board of directors' lack of independence	Limited review of transactions and sometimes setting aside their "Code of Ethics"
Greed, bonuses, and stock options	Collapse of business for short-term gains

Analysis

Over the past three decades, I have observed an interesting metamorphosis. As an independent auditor of U.S. public companies since 1981 and, presently, as an audit partner for a regional public accounting firm in California, I am often asked by clients to help them understand what is happening to their financial reporting systems.

Much of the financial crisis we've observed since the collapse of Enron is directly related to poor decision making regarding the accounting treatment for revenue recognition, off-balance sheet entities, cost capitalization, and stock options.

Prior to the recent rash of accounting failures, we had an early warning of the impending collapse of business ethics. In August 2000, the Panel on Audit Effectiveness (*O'Malley Report*) reported several weaknesses in the business auditing environment in the U.S. that speak out to the core of business ethics. The report noted the following:

> Earnings management also may involve intentionally recognizing or measuring transactions and other events and circumstances in the wrong accounting period or recording fictitious transactions—both of which constitute fraud. Choosing the appropriate period in which to recognize a transaction requires both management's and the auditor's understanding of all the relevant facts and circumstances.
>
> Earnings management that constitutes "fraud" is distinctly different from earnings management that is perceived as reducing the quality of earnings.
>
> The motivation to manage earnings comes in part from management's responsibility to direct the entity's operations in a way that achieves targeted results. The motivation also comes from pressures from management from sources both outside and inside the entity. External pressures come principally from the capital markets. Many observers believe that Wall Street's expectations significantly affect both appropriate and inappropriate management behaviors.
>
> Opportunity is a necessary feature of fraud, and it explains why management is in a unique position to perpetrate it. As the stewards of a corporate entity,

management possesses the power to manipulate the accounting records and prepare fraudulent financial reports. Whatever controls might be present in an entity, management has the ability to override them. Management can solicit whatever "help" it needs to carry out the fraud by directing or enlisting subordinates to assist. Thus, if collusion is needed to carry out the fraud, management can facilitate the collusion. If false documents need to be prepared, management can see that it is done. However, in those entities where the board of directors and management set the proper tone, promote high ethical standards and install appropriate controls to prevent and detect fraud, the opportunities to commit fraud can be reduced significantly.[3]

Biblical perspective

From a biblical perspective, good business ethics stem from godly counsel.

> Blessed is the man
> Who walks not in the counsel of the ungodly,
>> Nor stands in the path of sinners,
>> Nor sits in the seat of the scornful;
> But his delight is in the law of the LORD,
>> And in His law he meditates day and night.
> He shall be like a tree
>> Planted by the rivers of water,
>> That brings forth its fruit in its season,
>> Whose leaf also shall not wither;
> And *whatever he does shall prosper.*
>> —PSALM 1:1–3, EMPHASIS ADDED

Command those who are rich in this present age not to be haughty, nor to trust in uncertain riches

but in the living God, who gives us richly all things
to enjoy.

—1 Timothy 6:17

Although poor decision making has played a major role in today's
financial errors, the root cause of Corporate America's problems is a
lack of qualified ethics training and enforcement.

If a person is untrustworthy in small matters, he will be untrustworthy in greater areas.

> Unless you are faithful in small matters, you won't
> be faithful in large ones. If you cheat even a little,
> you won't be honest with greater responsibilities.
> And if you are untrustworthy about worldly wealth,
> who will trust you with the true riches of heaven?
>
> —Luke 16:10–11, nlt

Too often those who climb the corporate ladder do so by unlaw-
ful means, but that climb begins with a character flaw. Exaggerating
the numbers, lack of personal accountability, padding the expense
account, and so on are all part of the "forbidden fruit." The idea that
"no one is going to be hurt if I do this" is the rationalization.

FAILURE OF CORPORATE GOVERNANCE	
Problem	**Effect**
Lack of independence at the board level	Compromise on critical issues
Lack of detailed understanding of complex issues	"Off-balance sheet" transactions and others booked without oversight
Failure to hold management accountable	Limited review and questioning of complex arrangements

Analysis

Prior to the Enron debacle, boards of directors provided varying degrees of critical thinking and accountability for the CEO and senior management. The dozens of accounting failures since the fall of Enron strongly suggest that many directors did not do their jobs for the shareholders. In order for corporate governance to succeed, the boards of directors must be completely independent of the day-to-day operations of the company.

Nell Minow, cofounder and chairman of The Corporate Library, an independent investment research firm specializing in corporate governance and board effectiveness, has been a shareholders advocate for years. In an online article, "Company Response Report: CEO Contracts 1999," Ms. Minow highlights the "best and worst" CEO contracts for that year.

A CEO's employment contract is a public document, but it is sent to the SEC, and not to shareholders or included in their Form 10K annual report. Ms. Minow believes that such a document can provide key insights into the board's relationship with the CEO.[4]

> I really want to emphasize this point—the primary purpose of this compilation is to help us evaluate directors, not CEOs. We want CEOs to be aggressive and even a little greedy. But we depend on directors to make sure that those qualities are directed at shareholder value. It's fine for the CEO to ask for the moon. But it is the job of the directors to say, "Sure! You can have half of the moon now, and the other half when the stock price doubles."[5]

In their 1999 report, Global Crossing's CEO Robert Annunziata worked out a sweetheart deal at the expense of shareholders. Aside from his annual salary of $500,000, some of the "perks" were outrageous. For instance, he received a $10 million signing bonus and $2 million in stock options at $10 a share below market. The contract also provided the make and model of the Mercedes the company would purchase for him and included the provision to fly his family first class to visit him.

Ms. Minow gave her analysis of the situation:

> So, from that contract I concluded that a) the CEO thought the stock was going to decline in value and b) the board was incapable of saying no to him. But no one really took it very seriously.[6]

Biblical perspective

Over the past fourteen years, I had the opportunity to serve as the treasurer of a fascinating Christian school (K–12) overlooking the Pacific Ocean in Solana Beach, California. The school had started in the 1970s as an outreach ministry of a larger Christian school network in San Diego. By the mid-1980s the school became an independent educational institution. When I was appointed treasurer in the late 1980s, the school was struggling financially and was governed by a volunteer Board of Directors comprised of parents with a wide variety of backgrounds. Over the fourteen years I served on the board, I observed several trends:

- Asset growth from $2 million to over $18 million

- Equity from nil to over $12 million in fourteen years

- Positive growth in tuition, salaries, and quality of education

- Profitability and endowment funds that substantially improved its financial health

- Building additions and expansion of the campus with minimal debt

- Godly leadership at the top

Looking back at these phenomena, I noted four key elements to the school's success:

1. God's goodness and blessings were on this ministry.

2. There was increased emphasis on corporate governance.

3. The board of directors of the school was elected by the parents at annual "Town Hall Meetings" and served for specified terms. The commitment required substantial time and effort.

4. The annual Town Hall Meetings were an "open book" as to the financial position and always included a review of the school's audited financial statements. All key financial data were made available to all parents.

These board meetings were a good example of biblical accountability and governance and in-depth review of the strategic direction of the school within the biblical mandates of its charter.

The monthly board meetings were typically held in the evenings and would last from four to six hours and, at times, into the early morning hours of the next day. These meetings lasted so long because they wanted to make biblically based, sound decisions. The meetings opened with prayer and a time of Bible study and seeking God's guidance. These meetings represented a sincere attempt to provide biblically based decisions as a result of wise men and women wrestling with key issues. Today, Santa Fe Christian is one of the top Christian schools in the United States.

This fourteen-year experience was a good example of the kind of biblical corporate governance needed in America today. While not perfect, it went a long way toward that goal. The blessings and fruit of this obedience are evident on the Santa Fe campus today.

> If anyone wants to provide leadership in the church, good! But there are preconditions: A leader must be well-thought-of, committed to his wife, cool and collected, accessible, and hospitable. He must know what he's talking about, not be overfond of wine, not pushy but gentle, not thin-skinned, not money-hungry. He must handle his own affairs well, attentive to his own children and having their respect. For if someone is unable to handle his own affairs, how can he take care of God's church?
> —1 TIMOTHY 3:1–4, THE MESSAGE

Good corporate governance starts with ethical individuals who run their personal lives in a manner that honors God and can be trusted with greater responsibilities.

FAILURE IN THE AUDIT PROCESS/INDEPENDENCE	
PROBLEM	**EFFECT**
National firms changed their business model in the 1990s.	Audits were a "commodity."
Consulting fees greatly exceeded audit fees for most major clients.	Failure to act timely on risk assessment
Rule 203 of AICPA Code of Conduct was ignored.	Clean opinions should not have been issued when financial statements were misleading
Complexity of accounting issues/ audit team structure.	Detailed understanding of issues by the audit team was questionable.
Application of materiality rules was weak.	Too many waived audit adjustments
Record retention policies were fragmented.	Shredding documents and indictments

Analysis

The national accounting firms' movement in the 1980s and 1990s from strong "audit-driven" practices to "consulting-based" practices changed the focus of risk and emphasis on quality of the audits. In many cases this resulted in the loss of some independent thinking. Too often the auditors were too involved in the day-to-day operations, acting as consultants to senior management.

In the 1990s, the audits of public and private companies were viewed as "a commodity." Effectively, this reduced the perceived value of an audit to a lower level, both in the minds of the company's senior management and also in the minds of the auditors. The scope of the audit work and internal review of the audit documentation and process was reduced. Audit fees were inadequate to provide the true depth of review needed to evaluate the complexity of the corporate environments. The search for fraud was also limited by the then-existing auditing standards. Today the Statement of Auditing Standards No. 99 requires a much more proactive look for fraud. Currently the Public Company Accounting Oversight Board (PCAOB) *is* looking for increased scrutiny and fraud detection as it inspects the accounting firms and their audit work of public companies.

The November 2003 issue of the *Journal of Accounting* notes:

> Reestablishing integrity as the CPA's primary focus is Job No. 1—for the new AICPA Chairman S. Scott Voynich...noting that the CPA's most important asset is his or her reputation for honesty and fairness.[7]

Biblical perspective

> Except the LORD build the house, they labor in vain that build it.
> —PSALM 127:1, KJV

> Where there is no counsel, the people fall; But in the multitude of counselors there is safety.
> —PROVERBS 11:14

Having served as an audit/SEC partner in three multinational/ regional firms during the last thirty years in public accounting, I have observed from a spiritual perspective the following:

- The plethora of fraud and audit failures is much more substantial than most CPAs would have imagined.

- The effect of a lack of ethics training in the business schools is now evident to all.

- Greed within the accounting profession had replaced the standards of excellent once touted by the profession.

- The "overhaul" of the system is long overdue and will hopefully be addressed by the PCAOB's efforts to instill discipline.

- The reprogramming of auditors and their clients must occur soon, and the Sarbanes-Oxley Act opens the door to that possibility.

From a biblical perspective, this is effectively a time of repentance and Reformation in Corporate America. My hope is that the reader of this book will not only heed the call for reformation but also put it into action.

FAILURE OF AUDIT COMMITTEES	
Issues	**Effect**
Limited understanding of their role	Audit committee failed to perform on a timely basis.
Lack of detailed review of transactions	Independence compromised
Audit vs. consulting fees were out of balance.	Ignored signals of accounting problems
Lack of fraud-detection programs	"Go along" with management
Failure to speak up	Don't speak out; don't drill down in the details.

Analysis

Over the past thirty years in public accounting, I have spent a substantial amount of my professional career either (1) getting prepared for audit committee meetings, (2) attending audit committee meetings, or (3) reacting to decisions made in the audit committee meetings.

I also now serve as the audit committee chairman for a public pharmaceutical company and as their "financial expert" on the board of directors as required by SOX. So I can see the audit from both sides of the table.

Historically, the role of the audit committee had been one without a clear path and clear eligibility requirements. Many audit committees were comprised of individuals who did not have the following:

- A thorough understanding of Generally Accepted Accounting Principles (GAAP) and current developments in the ever-changing world of accounting

- An understanding of how to work with the independent accounting firms and their requirements under GAAS (General Accepted Auditing Standards)

- A clear understanding of the relationships between the committee and the CFO and CEO

The role of the audit committee and its chairperson is critical to the Reformation of Corporate America. It is here that accountability for audit performance is maintained and communicated to management and the board of directors. Audit committees must have members who have substantial accounting, auditing, and financial backgrounds.

An article in *CFO Magazine* stated:

> Growing numbers of financial accounting experts believe that GAAP itself may be part of the [audit failure] problem. As financial transactions have become more complicated, so, too, has the accounting for them. "Over the last 10 years, U.S. GAAP has evolved into complex detailed rules that encourage financial engineering rather than transparency," says DiPiazza [global CEO of PwC].
>
> GAAP has enabled companies to comply with the accounting standards and yet violate basic principles of transparency and risk disclosure.[8]

So, what is the solution? According to DiPiazza, "principles."

> It's a lot harder for me to bend a principle than to bend a rule," says DiPiazza. [9]

The article went on to say that DiPiazza:

> …believes the International Accounting Standards movement, which relies more on a principles-based framework, can provide momentum for a similar approach in the United States….Regulators may not

be inclined to rely on the good judgment of auditors at this point, but *integrity and adherence to principles are the only things that will restore confidence in the audit community and in financial disclosures.*[10]

—EMPHASIS ADDED

While audit committee members must have a thorough knowledge of accounting and auditing processes, it is also extremely important that they practice integrity in their committee.

Biblical perspective

The biblical perspective to this failure relies on the very concept upon which the accounting industry was founded—*principles* and *integrity.*

It is like a person who builds a house *on a strong foundation* laid upon the underlying rock. When the floodwaters rise and break against the house, *it stands firm because it is well built.* But anyone who listens and doesn't obey is like a person who builds a house without a foundation. When the floods sweep down against that house, *it will crumble into a heap of ruins.*

—LUKE 6:48–49, NLT, EMPHASIS ADDED

The audit committee must serve as the "nerve center" for ethics related to the financial elements of a company. Accordingly, the integrity and technical training of the chairman and each member of the committee are paramount.

Here are the keys to a strong, biblically based audit committee:

1. Audit committee charters based on ethics derived from a biblical model of what is "right" and "wrong"

2. Committee members who are committed to the time and sacrifice needed to be effective

and who are willing to invest in the technical training efforts to stay current on audit
and accounting issues

3. Frequent meetings to address the regulatory
   needs of the company and to stay in close communication with the CFO/corporate controller

4. Frequent meetings with the independent
   accountants to address issues of concern and
   establish an atmosphere that encourages the
   audit partner to discuss freely any concerns
   that he has about the registrant and its
   personnel

5. Establishment of a continuing education
   procedure for the audit committee to maintain technical excellence

6. Periodic training for the rest of the board
   of directors to keep them aware of key accounting concepts and assist them with their
   review of financial data

7. Committee members' willingness and ability
   to review key transactions and look at potential fraud at all areas of the enterprise

UNMANAGEABLE COMPLEXITY OF TRANSACTIONS	
Issues	**Effect**
Trillions of dollars in derivative transactions	Stress on accounting systems
SPEs (Special Purpose Entities)	Application of very complex rules is risky.
Derivatives Accounting	795 pages of detailed "rules-based" accounting—FASB 133
Billions of dollars in accounting errors	Restatement of many financial statements

Analysis

The complex U.S. economy and the plethora of complex accounting rules have left our nation drowning in rules and few who really understand them. Providing an audit these days seems like a daunting task for any auditor given the additional requirements of the Sarbanes-Oxley Act and the potential new standards to be set by the PCAOB.

The accounting department and external auditing foundations are more demanding than at any time in history. The resources and attitudes toward the accounting function and the related auditors (both internal and external) must be substantially increased to prevent the failures of the past.

Many industry professionals believe part of the solution is for auditors to hire veterans to work more "onsite" on the riskier audits than hiring college graduates.[11]

> Robert Halliday, CFO of Varian Semiconductor Equipment Associates Inc., in Gloucester, Massachusetts, thinks auditors can't be skeptical if they don't understand what they're looking at. "They have so much mechanical work—no one

stands back, thinks about it, and asks, 'Does all this make sense?'" he says. "But auditors can only do that if they have experience or if they know the industry. Gray hair is helpful."

"When people say that audit quality has decreased, that's what they're talking about— less-experienced people," says Frank Borelli [former CFO of Marsh & McLennan Cos. and chairman of the Express Scripts Inc. audit committee]. "We have to have specialist auditors who know the industry from a high level of experience, and these are the people who should be supervising the audits instead of selling new business."[12]

There is something to be said of those who have more experience in life. From a biblical perspective, the solution to managing the complexity of accounting rules *and* complying with government regulations rests with a multitude of independent counselors and elders.

Biblical perspective

The Old Testament gives us examples of how "executives" were elected and craftsmen were divinely appointed.

> And Moses said to the children of Israel. "See, the LORD has called by name Bezalel the son of Uri, the son of Hur, of the tribe of Judah; and *He has filled him with the Spirit of God, in wisdom and understanding, in knowledge and all manner of workmanship.* . . . And Bezalel and Aholiab, and every gifted artisan in whom *the LORD has put wisdom and understanding, to know how to do all manner of work for the service of the sanctuary,* shall do according to all that the LORD has commanded.
> —EXODUS 35:30–31; 36:1, EMPHASIS ADDED

Employment skills are God-given, and He is the One who enhances them for the work at hand. These two men, Bezalel and Aholiab, were placed as "general overseers," but they also worked, taught those less experienced (Exod. 35:34), and gave account for the materials used in this building project.

> Here is an inventory of the materials used in building the Tabernacle of the Covenant. Moses directed the Levites *to compile the figures,* and Ithamar son of Aaron the priest *served as recorder.* Bezalel son of Uri, grandson of Hur, of the tribe of Judah, *was in charge of the whole project,* just as the LORD had commanded Moses. *He was assisted by Oholiab son of Ahisamach, of the tribe of Dan, a craftsman expert.*
>
> —EXODUS 38:21–23, NLT, EMPHASIS ADDED

God is a God of order, not confusion. (See 1 Corinthians 14:33.) Auditing practices existed even in ancient times. Bezalel, as "CEO," and Oholiab, as "manager," gave an account of all materials to the "auditor" or "gatekeeper" Ithamar—an independent source with no direct ties. It was Ithamar who then needed to bring the "audit" to Moses, "chairman of the board."

God chose experienced men, filled them with His Spirit to enhance their natural abilities, commanded them to train the inexperienced, and held them accountable for the "inventory."

Even today under SOX, the same mandate for "experience" is very clear. Look at the SOX requirements for the "Audit Committee Financial Expert":

- An understanding of GAAP financial statements

- The ability to assess the application of GAAP to the accounting for estimates, accruals, and reserves

- Experience preparing, auditing, analyzing, or evaluating (or actively supervising these activities) financial statements with a breadth and level of complexity of accounting issues that are comparable to the registrant's statements

- An understanding of audit committee functions

The audit committee financial expert is to have acquired the above attributes through:

- Education and experience as (or active supervision of) a principal financial officer, principal accounting officer, controller, public accountant or auditor, or experience in one or more positions that involve the performance of similar functions

- Experience overseeing or assessing the performance of companies or public accountants with respect to the preparation, auditing, or evaluation of financial statements.

WALL STREET PRESSURES	
Issues	**Effect**
Investment bankers' demands	Rush to announce quarterly results
Continued need to generate fees	Investment bankers' excessive profits
Complex structures	Lack of substance over form

Analysis

Wall Street and its desire for quarterly corporate profits place tremendous pressure on U.S. public companies. Wall Street often focuses on short-term profits versus long-term values. The model is broken and is quite contrary to the biblical model for businesses.

One of the fundamental flaws in the U.S. economy is the intense focus on the amount of short-term "quarterly" earnings. While it is important to understand how a company is doing periodically, the "maddening environment" in which we operate today is one in which a company's stock price and market capitalization are almost entirely dependent on what happened in the last ninety days!

Such a myopic approach puts tremendous pressure on earnings/loss results with limited value attributed to building a company with strong internal accounting controls, IT systems, and ethics training.

In 2000, the *O'Malley Report* noted that many observers believe that Wall Street's expectations significantly affect both appropriate and inappropriate management behaviors.[13] In his speech "The Numbers Game," former SEC chairman Arthur Levitt observed:

> Increasingly, I have become concerned that the motivation to meet Wall Street earnings expectations may be overriding common sense business practices. . . . As a result, I fear that we are witnessing erosion in the quality of earnings, and therefore, the quality of financial reporting. . . . Many in Corporate

America are just as frustrated and concerned about
this trend as we, at the SEC, are. They know how
difficult it is to hold the line on good practices when
their competitors operate in the gray area between
legitimacy and outright fraud.[14]

Over my years in public accounting, I have often experienced
very tight time pressures of mandated and artificial deadlines. The
Wall Street pressure is always there and, in many cases, is not moti-
vated by the desire to get the "numbers right." Is this environment
healthy? Many poor decisions are made late in the day, under pressure, and regrettably, many should never have been made in that
frame of mind. Even in Genesis 2, we see that God rested on the
seventh day.

What is occurring in the U.S. under SOX should be encouraging. In the October 2003 newsletter *The Practicing CPA,* issued by
the AICPA Alliance for CPA firms, it was noted that:

> For both public and private firms, the foremost
> challenge may well be to ensure that chief execu-
> tives and financial officers avoid the risks associated
> with Section 302 of Sarbanes-Oxley, which man-
> dates that they certify their companies' financial
> statements, and with Section 404, which requires
> management to report on the effectiveness of their
> internal financial controls and outside auditors to
> attest to the management reports. CPA firms are
> helping with the internal controls assessments that
> other companies' auditors are prohibited from as-
> sisting in.[15]

Biblical perspective

> Better a little with righteousness than much gain
> with injustice.
>
> —PROVERBS 16:8, NIV

> The trustworthy will get a rich reward, but the person who wants to get rich quick will only get into trouble.
>
> —Proverbs 28:20, NLT

> When people do not accept divine guidance, they run wild. But whoever does the law is happy.
>
> —Proverbs 29:18, NLT

The 1980s and 1990s were decades built around short-term earnings and price spikes. Wall Street often failed to look at long-term investments and long-term trends. Companies with substantial core businesses that yielded respectable returns were not in vogue. The key to long-term financial health is building a strong foundation, adding layers of business as appropriate to build a high-quality enterprise to provide goods and services needed by God's creation.

| FAILURE OF DISCLOSURES IN PUBLIC DOCUMENTS ||
Issues	Effect
Form 10K/10Q disclosures were limited in certain instances.	Investors and employees were not aware of the seriousness of problems on a timely basis.
Internal accounting control's testing was limited in the 1990s.	Material weaknesses went undetected.
SEC reporting requirements needed to be enhanced.	Substantial changes to MD&A and timely disclosure of executive/director equity transactions (post SOX)

Analysis

While many shareholders fail to read thoroughly the available SEC filings of public registrants, the accuracy of some of the disclosures was questionable. The lack of clarity in the Enron financial statements regarding the off-balance sheet liabilities was a great example.

The need for more detail of complex transactions has been very clear with the unveiling of the multitude of accounting failures. In particular, off-balance sheet activity and derivatives have been key areas of concern and abuse.

Some critics of the state of auditing don't blame the auditors as much as the financial reporting that they have to work with in today's environment. Walter P. Schuetze, former SEC chief accountant and chairman of two audit committees, says that as long as management is allowed to estimate so much of a financial statement, auditors' hands will be tied.[16]

Biblical perspective

> But we have renounced the hidden things of shame, not walking in craftiness nor handling the word of God deceitfully, but by manifestation of the truth commending ourselves to every man's conscience in the sight of God.
>
> —2 CORINTHIANS 4:2

> It is better to be poor and honest than to be a fool and dishonest.
>
> —PROVERBS 19:1, NLT

> You can make many plans; but the LORD's purpose will prevail.
>
> —PROVERBS 19:21, NLT

Ultimately, the truth will always percolate to the surface, sometimes rapidly, or as in the case of Enron and others, it may take years, but it will occur at some time and in some way.

| FAILURE IN ACCOUNTING AND REPORTING MODELS ||
Problem	Effect
FASB consolidation project delayed	SPE Accounting and Consolidation Accounting revisited after Enron
Rules-setting organizations under political pressure	"Rules-Based" Model is subject to much concern.
"U.S. GAAP" Model is questioned	International GAAP— "Principles-Based" Model gains strength.

Analysis

While the Financial Accountants Standards Board (FASB) and Emerging Issues Task Force (EITF) have done an outstanding job in many respects over the years, their lengthy "due process" for issuing statements and outside political pressures have taken a toll on addressing certain accounting issues on a timely basis prior to Enron. Since the Enron debacle, the PCAOB, SEC, FASB, and EITF have moved quickly to fill the following gaps:

- Auditor independence

- Auditor oversight

- Expanded auditing standards

- Focus on fraud detection

- Revised emphasis on internal controls

- Limitations on scope of services by the outside accountants

- Audit partner rotation

Enron, WorldCom, Adelphia, and others have triggered substantial changes to the accounting and auditing profession in the following areas:

- Increased scrutiny of derivative accounting

- Strict application of revenue recognition rules

- The accounting treatment for stock options

- The accounting treatment for off-balance sheet entities

- Adequacy of internal accounting controls

The FASB and EITF have addressed many of these issues with the following:

> In July 2002, the FASB issued Statement of Financial Accounting Standards No. 146 (SFAS No. 146) and "Accounting for Costs Associated with Exit or Disposal Activities" (effective January 1, 2003). SFAS No. 146 replaces current accounting literature and requires the recognition of costs associated with exit or disposal activities when they are incurred rather than at the date of a commitment to an exit or disposal plan.
>
> In November 2002, the FASB issued FASB Interpretation No. 45, "Guarantor's Accounting and Disclosure Requirements for Guarantees, Including Indirect Guarantees of Indebtedness of Others." This interpretation addressed the disclosures to be made by a guarantor in its interim and annual financial statements about its obligations and guarantees. This interpretation also clarifies the requirements related to the recognition of a liability by a guarantor at the inception of a guarantee for the obligations that the guarantor has undertaken in issuing that guarantee.
>
> In December 2002, the FASB issued SFAS No. 148, "Accounting for Stock-Based Compensation—

Transition and Disclosure." This statement amends FASB Statement No. 123 to provide alternative methods of transition for a voluntary change to the fair-value-based method of accounting for stock-based employee compensation. In addition, the statement amends the disclosure requirements of Statement No. 123 to require prominent disclosures in both annual and interim financial statements about the method of accounting for stock-based employee compensation and the effect of the method used on reported results.

In January 2003, the FASB issued Interpretation No. 46, "Consolidation of Variable Interest Entities." This interpretation clarifies the application of Accounting Research Bulletin No. 51, "Consolidated Financial Statement," to certain entities in which equity investors do not have the characteristics of a controlling financial interest or do not have sufficient equity at risk for the entity to finance its activities without additional subordinated financial support from other parties. It further clarifies whether an entity should be subject to consolidation according to the provisions of this interpretation, if by design, certain conditions exist.

Today there is substantial pressure on the U.S. accounting standard setting and regulatory bodies to converge with the new International Accounting Standards, which will be implemented in 2005 in the European Union. This will be a dramatic era of change: a shift from "rules-based" to "principle-based" accounting models.

Biblical perspective

It is very important that accounting models reflect the truth about the economics and substance of transactions.

The trustworthy will get a rich reward. But the person who wants to get rich quick will only get into trouble.

—PROVERBS 28:20, NLT

Through wise and godly counsel accounting professionals can reflect an entity's financial status in a manner that reflects the truth.

Blinding Arrogance	
Problem	**Effect**
Senior management was not held accountable by the board of directors.	Board of directors failed the shareholders.
National accounting firms focused on their consulting practices.	Audit practices suffered.
Fast-paced corporate environments left little time to evaluate transactions thoroughly.	"Go with the flow" mentality took over.

Analysis

The pre-Enron era was marked with a generation of businesses that were "high" on their new Internet-based models and generated a sense that sound financial concepts were no longer applicable.

The 1990s were a decade of extreme growth in revenue and utilization of capital, particularly venture capital and IPO funds. The growth and profits brought forth an "invincible attitude" that lifted many "above the law."

The day after WorldCom Inc. admitted cooking its books to the tune of $3.8 billion, former Andersen Worldwide CEO Joseph F. Berardino was glued to the TV set watching CNBC's coverage of the shocking news. Berardino had good reason to be riveted to every development: WorldCom was a major audit client of the firm he had recently quit.

Like the rest of the world, Berardino watched in outrage. But in his case, the ire was directed at the media, which he believed was exaggerating the story. "They were talking down the market," says Berardino with disgust. Four weeks later, the beleaguered telecom provider filed the largest bankruptcy in U.S. history.

Berardino seemed clueless as to how Andersen could have failed to detect the fraud at WorldCom, which occurred over five consecutive quarters. "In a quarter, you're typically not looking at that kind of detail," he says. "It's shocking. It just blows your mind. But why was that stock down to $1 already? It's because some investors did their homework."

Of course many are wondering if Berardino, who resigned in disgrace as CEO in March, had done this. At 51, he finds himself exiled from the industry that consumed him for nearly 30 years, a mere bystander to a national debate that will result in the most sweeping reform of the profession he worked in all of his adult life.[17]

Biblical perspective

The plans of the diligent lead to profit as surely as haste leads to poverty.

—PROVERBS 21:5, NIV

If you need wisdom—if you want to know what God wants you to do—ask him, and he will gladly tell you. He will not resent your asking.

—JAMES 1:5, NLT

This attitude and arrogance are exemplified in a *Forbes* July 22, 2002 article by Daniel Lyons entitled "Bad Boys."

At some point, though, morals count for something. Many companies face the dilemma: If a top producer gets in an embarrassing scrape, should he be fired? What if a terrific salesman cheats on his expense account, or a key executive is sued for sexual harassment or arrested for drunk driving? To set the threshold of indignation too high runs the risk that the miscreant's next misdeed will cost your company a devastating legal settlement. To set it too low means losing talent to a rival.[18]

| FAILURE TO LISTEN TO EARLY WARNING SIGNS ||
Problem	Effect
Whistle blowers were ignored.	Failure to report on a timely basis
Auditors ignored certain input from outside sources.	Didn't listen to the messenger adequately

Analysis

Like Noah and the Flood, a number of people communicated clearly that serious problems lay ahead. The corporate world was unprepared and unwilling to receive the messages and was often harsh on the whistleblower. Congress gave the SEC power via the Sarbanes-Oxley Act to protect the whistleblower as follows.

SOX Provides the Following Procedures for Handling Complaints

The audit committee must place some reliance on management for information about the company's financial reporting process. Since the audit committee is dependent to a degree on the information provided to it by management and internal and outside auditors, it is imperative for the committee to cultivate open and effective channels of information. Management may not have the appropriate incentives to self-report all questionable practices. A company employee or other individual may be reticent to report concerns regarding questionable accounting or other matters for fear of management reprisal. The establishment of formal procedures for receiving and handling complaints should serve to facilitate disclosures, encourage proper individual conduct and alert the audit committee to potential problems before they have serious consequences.

Accordingly, under the listing standards called for by our final rules, each audit committee must establish procedures for: the receipt, retention and treatment of complaints received by the issuer regarding accounting, internal accounting controls or auditing matters, and the confidential, anonymous submission by employees of the issuer of concerns regarding questionable accounting or auditing matters.

... Given the variety of listed issuers in the U.S. capital markets, we believe audit committees should be provided with flexibility to develop and utilize procedures appropriate for their circumstances. The procedures that will be most effective to meet the requirements for a very small listed issuer with few employees could be very different from the processes and systems that would need to be in place for large, multi-national corporations with thousands of employees in many different jurisdictions. We do not believe that in this instance a "one-size-fits-all" approach would be appropriate. As noted in the Proposing Release, we expect each audit committee to develop procedures that work best consistent with its company's individual circumstances to meet the requirements in the final rule. Similarly, we are not adopting the suggestion of a few commenters that, despite the statutory language, the requirement should be limited to only employees in the financial reporting area.[19]

Listed issuers must comply with this rule by October 31, 2004. Foreign private and small business issuers' deadline to comply is July 31, 2005.

It is in management's best interest to listen to whistleblowers and then react appropriately.

A recent example of the importance of this legislation is as follows:

> When Matthew Whitley was laid off from his job last March as a finance manager at The Coca-Cola Co., along with about 1,000 other employees, he didn't take it lying down. Two months later, Whitley approached his former employer seeking a whopping settlement—$44.4 million—on the grounds that he had been fired in retaliation for raising concerns about accounting fraud. When Coke balked, Whitley turned for relief to a new ally: The Sarbanes-Oxley Act of 2002. He filed for whistle-blower protection under the act's Section 806 provisions, and initiated federal and state lawsuits that charged seven Coke executives, including CFO Gary Fayard, with crimes ranging from racketeering to mail and wire fraud.
>
> "This disgruntled former employee has made a number of allegations accompanied by an ultimatum: that the company pay him almost $45M or he would go to the media," said Coke in a May

statement announcing the claims. Since then, a Georgia State court judge has dismissed most of the charges, including those related to racketeering and breaches of fiduciary responsibility. While Coke may still have to defend itself against claims related to wrongful termination, "we are confident we will prevail once the facts are presented in a court of law," said Coke in a statement.

One of Whitley's allegations, however, has already had some effect. His contention that Coke falsified a marketing test of Frozen Coke at Burger King restaurants in Virginia led the company to make a public apology and an offer to pay Burger King $21 million. In July, the Department of Justice (DOJ) announced it was launching a criminal investigation of the alleged fraud.[20]

Biblical perspective

Applying godly principles can pay, and will pay, dividends to those who choose to follow the principles. The companies that exhibit the best corporate governance are posed for growth

> Trust in the LORD with all your heart, and lean not on your own understanding; in all your ways acknowledge Him, and He shall direct your paths.
>
> —PROVERBS 3:5–6

This ten-point analysis is helpful in establishing understanding what has happened since the collapse of Enron and the avalanche of accounting failures and fraud. Hopefully, it provides some boundaries for avoiding the pitfalls of erroneous accounting. In the next chapter we will look at specific modern-day cases—good and poor examples—of corporate integrity or lack thereof.

We are careful to be honorable before the Lord, but we also want everyone else to know we are honorable.

—2 CORINTHIANS 8:21, NLT

CHAPTER 2

"Tone at the Top"

Our vision of America is one of free enterprise tempered by accountability; a nation built with the best judicial system in the world with a multi-trillion dollar economy and superpower status. And yet where were the auditors and our ethics in this period of corporate meltdown? As we look for a bridge to a new era, an era of reformation built on a historic Christian ethic, we must further analyze what has happened to us in the last two decades.

Since beginning my career in public accounting in the mid-1970s, I have observed a pronounced migration in the public accounting industry. This industry has gone from one that reviewed internal accounting controls thoroughly and conducted very detailed auditing of most clients to a culture characterized by a "substantive year-end-testing approach" and a lot of pressure to sell "other services" from the firms' consulting menu.

During the 1990s, the public accounting model changed dramatically and the audit/attestation portion of the business took a back seat to the consultants in the industry. In fact, during the late 1990s and early 2000s, the American Institute of Certified Public Accounts (AICPA) worked hard to promote credentials other than those specific to the audit industry.

Barbara Ley Toffler in her book *Final Accounting: Ambition, Greed and the Fall of Arthur Andersen* discussed the slow evolution within Arthur Andersen that shifted the power base from the audit partners to the consultants over several years.[1] In 2002, that accounting firm collapsed under the weight of the audit failures at Sunbeam, Waste Management, and Enron.

The litigation and audit failures for the period of 1999–2004 have been astounding and monumental. The desire for larger partner incomes and the leveraging of audit staff beyond levels that afforded good supervision and thorough reviews of their work products contributed greatly to these severe problems in the public accounting industry.

Without a great deal of fanfare, the "Tone at the Top" of many corporations and public accounting firms changed. I saw it in my clients and in the accounting firms I worked for—a strong desire for doing what was right was not the focus of many clients. I always felt that someday there would be a price to pay.

Corporate America in Financial Crisis

For the sake of simplicity, let's look at three companies that lacked ethical values and paid the consequences, and three companies with biblical values ingrained in their company's mission statements.

WorldCom

The WorldCom case is an interesting one. WorldCom represents the largest corporate bankruptcy in U.S. history to date. The company reported approximately $80 billion worth of assets—including goodwill and other intangible assets—deemed worthless on its balance sheet. (The initial detection of account irregularities was $11 billion, only a fraction of what was ultimately reported.)

The WorldCom case also set into motion the review of other telecom company asset valuations (e.g., Qwest Communications and Global Crossing). Both companies have experienced substantial difficulties as a result of WorldCom.

As noted in chapter three, "The Psychology of Fraud," the perception of fraud at WorldCom, in the minds of certain accounting professionals, was not a "planned event"; rather, it occurred when individuals were confronted with a basic question: What is the right course of action?

The *Wall Street Journal* reported on June 23, 2003, that one of WorldCom's accountants, Betty Vinson, at first balked at the idea of cooking the books. But her loyalty to the company and inability to separate right from wrong led her to cave in to the demands of her superiors. Having caved once, it was a little easier the next three quarters of 2001, until she could do this no more. She ultimately confessed to the federal authorities and pleaded guilty to two criminal counts of conspiracy and securities fraud.[2] In the spring of 2002, CFO Scott Sullivan and the Director of General Accounting at WorldCom were indicted.

Peregrine Systems, Inc.

My firm, Swenson Advisors, LLP, had the unique opportunity to provide substantial assistance in the cleanup of the accounting records of this international software company in 2002. It stands today as the largest bankruptcy of a software company in the history of the United States to date. This was a software company that touted rapid growth and frequent acquisitions as a key to its success. Take a look at some of the highlights of the case:

- Arthur Andersen was the independent public accounting firm before the bankruptcy.

- The company restated previously reported revenue of $1.34 billion for the period from April 1, 1999 through December 31, 2001, off by $509 million, representing an amazing 48 percent misstatement of revenue.[3]

- In the spring of 2003, the company's CFO pled guilty to committing securities fraud, and the company's vice president of sales followed suit.[4]

- Hundreds of employees' lives were deeply impacted by this loss of employment and stock options value.

It should be noted that Peregrine has emerged from bankruptcy, a smaller company that continues to market its software products.

HealthSouth

One of the trends in public accounting in the 1990s that derailed the industry was the focus on consulting fees versus audit fees. HealthSouth, a Birmingham, Alabama-based healthcare service provider with operations throughout the U.S., is just one example of this type of accounting fraud. As a result, the company also experienced the following:

- The SEC has accused the company of massive accounting fraud resulting in a $1.4 billion overstatement of revenue.

- The SEC accused the HealthSouth chairman of meeting regularly with the CFO to inflate earnings to make Wall Street estimates.

- The former CFO (as well as others) plead guilty to SEC accusations in March 2003.

- Ernst and Young reported substantial fees from the company in excess of the basic audit services fees.[5]

Corporate Integrity Leads to Peace and Prosperity

In contrast to the examples of how corruption leads to chaos and poverty, take a closer look at examples of corporate integrity at work.

Eagle Plastics and Rubber

A pleasant fall day in October 2003 afforded the opportunity to dedicate a newly formed business facility that recycles rubber products. Eagle Plastics and Rubber (Eagle), a division of AeroPro LLC, in eastern Tennessee, opened their doors with a ceremony that featured a bold display of integrity to its employees and to community leaders in attendance. Patriotism, prayer, community service, and a communication of Christian values are all part of Eagle's foundation. Their motto is "In God Is Our Trust," and the company's adopted Bible verse is Hebrews 3:4, which says, "For every house is built by some man; but he that built all things is God" (KJV).

The following is a portion of Eagle's mission statement:

AEROPRO IS COMMITTED TO THE FOLLOWING:

- No matter how large or small the task, we will finish the job by setting obtainable goals.

- We will maintain an enthusiastic attitude toward each other and the work before us.

- Our goal is to do the job right the first time.

- We are determined to put others first. As we give of ourselves our blessings increase in proportion.

- Our mission is to perform every task to the best of our ability. Finding fault is easy. Fixing the problem is hard. We choose to put our best efforts into customer satisfaction. Our success as a company and as individuals depends on it.

What a contrast to the mind-set of many in today's corporate world who look for ways to exclude and circumvent ethics in their business environment. The owner and founder of AeroPro, Dan Ford, would be the first to admit that he had not always been guided by those standards of integrity in business, but embracing these values now has brought peace and honor into his life. "Those who listen to instruction will prosper; those who trust the LORD will be happy" (Proverbs 16:20, NLT).

Chick-fil-A

Chick-fil-A is an example of a workplace environment where Christian business ethics and care for the employees are at work. This company's founder and CEO, Truett Cathy, has been a testimony to employee relationships for years. The company's Web site proudly displays the following:

CLOSED SUNDAYS.
IT'S A PART OF THE CHICK-FIL-A RECIPE.

Admittedly, closing all of our restaurants every Sunday makes us a rarity in this day and age. But it's a little habit that has always served us well, so we're planning to stick with it.

Our founder, Truett Cathy, wanted to ensure that every Chick-fil-A employee and restaurant operator had an opportunity to worship, spend time with family and friends or just plain rest from the work week. Made sense then and still makes sense now.[6]

Some might say that it's ludicrous to close on Sunday, especially in the restaurant business, but not for Mr. Cathy. On the contrary, Chick-fil-A has prospered since first opening for business in 1967. In 2000, the company surpassed $1 billion in system-wide sales.[7]

Berryman & Henigar

Mr. Ray Berryman, founder and CEO of Berryman & Henigar, one of the leading civil engineering companies in the United States, has been a strong advocate for applying Christian values to the working lives of his employees for years. Without hesitation, Ray sets forth his biblical values in the company's mission statement as follows:

MISSION

Our mission is to honor God in all we do, to practice servant leadership, to serve our clients with superior quality service, and to provide our associates with development, opportunity, encouragement and appreciation.

VISION

Our vision is to be the recognized leader in serving public agencies by organizing our firm to be a consulting city, understanding the uniqueness and purpose of our clients, and providing them superior quality services with integrity guided by the practical application of biblical values.

VALUES

- Conduct our business with integrity based on biblical values.

- Practice the Golden Rule in all of our operations and relationships.

- Provide fabled (superior) service to our clients.

- Esteem, treasure, and respect each of our associates.

- Facilitate teamwork and unity.

- Practice servant leadership throughout all levels of our enterprise.

- Encourage growth and entrepreneurial leadership.

- Provide an excellent and wholesome working environment.

- Maintain profitability in each sector at acceptable levels to ensure good financial health.

- Enjoy what we do, and have fun doing it.

These companies, Eagle, Chick-Fil-A, and Berryman & Henigar, represent a wide range of industries. However, they have one theme in common: integrity in the workplace and respect for biblical values.

"Tone at the Top" is all about leadership. The many failures we see in the business press today represent the "hearts" of men, women, and organizations who did not embrace integrity. It is this period of repentance and remorse we are experiencing today that will provide the opportunity to be stronger in the future.

> When the godly are in authority, the people rejoice.
> But when the wicked are in power, they groan.
> —Proverbs 29:2, nlt

"Tone at the Top" can work for you. Godly leadership will provide the bridge to a healthier Corporate America. It will not be perfect, but the pain and discipline we are experiencing today mandate it!

Obviously, not all businesses hold the strong Judeo-Christian values represented in the previously mentioned corporations. One could safely assume, however, that there are many who strive to conduct their business affairs with some degree of integrity. It is not likely that a business owner would purposely set out to discredit himself or his company, especially in light of today's spotlight on the corporate world. Many do, however, and unfortunately are unable to reverse the unfortunate consequences. What happens through the course of time that creates such a change of direction in the lives and hearts of these professionals? What makes a man or woman abandon values they once embraced with a passion?

The next chapter answers many of those questions and provides insight into the "why" of fraudulent misconduct. We will take a deeper look into the "Tone at the Top" and understand what drives corruption in certain organizations.

Things gained through unjust fraud are never secure.[1]

—SOPHOCLES (497–406/5 B.C.),
GREEK TRAGEDIAN,
OEDIPUS COLONUS, L. 1026.

CHAPTER 3

The Psychology of Fraud— by Barry Minkow

~⌒

As we look to the future and the Reformation of Corporate America, it's very important to understand the mind-set of those who got us to where we are today. Barry Minkow has seen both sides of the table, and today is helping many in Corporate America change their hearts.

—STEVE AUSTIN

~⌒

Since the fall of 2001, the business press has rarely gone a day without screaming headlines about some type of serious fraud in financial reporting, workmen's compensation, medical billings, clinical trials for drug discovery, and even the preparation of résumés. How does this occur with such frequency in a nation that was once held as a sterling example of honest business practices in the global economy?

In the late 1990s, two Sony Pictures publicists created a fictitious film critic, whom they named David Manning, and placed him as part of an actual publication for which they worked. They attributed quotes in praise of some Sony films that were not so good (at least to the public), all to increase the movies' revenues. What was the outcome of this seemingly harmless deceit? Investors were not losing money, and the public remains largely unaffected; at least that is the rationalization. It was a creative advertising scam.[2]

In the pre-Enron era, the words *scam* and *fraud* were synonymous with illegal. Today, the devaluation of these terms has led straight to apathy. This apathy is directed at *why* people perpetrate these crimes in the first place, not at the victims of fraud. In reality, fraud undermines the American economy with devastating effects. The most neglected question in forensic accounting and fraud prevention (and detection) is, *Why?*

Why would intelligent men and women, with great resources and various options, resort to committing devastating crimes? What risk is worth the consequences? Family? Freedom or reputation? Even movie studios will attempt to deceive the masses for a box office hit. What is the motive behind this action?

The business of fraud rakes in about $400 billion per year (*six times the annual cost of operating the U.S. criminal justice system*).[3] Most accountants, bankers, and other professionals feel they know their clients well and do not worry about misrepresentation or deliberate fraud. They submit, "This could never happen to me or my firm. We only deal with *honest* people." Often times this statement is true. However, our penitentiary system is littered with white-collar criminals who have one thing in common: they committed fraud. None of them suspected they would be serving time for their misdeeds.

Talk to any corporate executive who committed a white-collar crime, and you'll hear the same story. None of them ever dreamed that a lengthy jail term would abruptly halt their business careers.

People don't set out to engage in illegal activities. At one point in their careers, good intentions were compromised for a simple shortcut to instant (yet fleeting) success or quick profits. Bit by bit, they compromised their integrity. Those initial good intentions may still be intact, but the method of achievement became unscrupulous.

Like robbery or murder, fraud requires an intent to deceive. No one intentionally sets out to commit actions that will ultimately incarcerate them. When the world of banking and accounting concede this point, the battle is halfway over. Why? Because now every partner in an accounting firm and prospective lenders will realize the best client with seemingly high morals is capable of the unimaginable. It is important to acknowledge a balance here. I'm not advocating a witch hunt of every client. Fraud is not lurking behind every balance sheet. Enough damage has been done, however, to take it seriously. When you understand the motive and psychology behind fraud, you will see how easy someone can be lured into the trap of fraudulent crime. Unfortunately, it is a self-created mousetrap.

Right Equals Forward Motion

We live in an age riddled with varying shades of color. No more black and white, right or wrong. The word *character* once meant "someone with moral or ethical standards." A person with "character" attracted accountants, bankers, and other business professionals.

However, a startling new philosophy has emerged from the business (and academic) sector. It is subtly attacking moral character by commonplace practice. This new ethic is called "*right equals forward motion.*" Best summarized in one word, right equals forward motion is about *achievement*. This has been a driving force behind much of the fraud in the United States.

The goal, or achievement, reigns over the strategy to reach it. *What you do* is more important than *who you are*. Anything that keeps you from achievement is wrong. Conversely, anything to accomplish that goal is right.

In an age of technology, deception is all too easy to conceal. For example, the college student who uses the Internet to complete assignments or download exams is cheating. The student's payoff is a degree. How will society view this individual? As a college graduate. How the graduate obtained the diploma is irrelevant. Hence, character takes a bow to the "new achievement ethic."

Consider this contemporary example. A partner in a large accounting firm must bill a certain amount of hours each month. He is competitive and wants to set the standard for everyone else—managers included. After all, hard work pays off. He is an honest man, but he is distressed to find his billable hours below average. His first-class plane trip spent in slumber now becomes billable time to a client. Although this example would fall into the soft fraud category, it is often practiced and boldly represents the term "right equals forward motion." Several of the national accounting firms have been sued over potential fraud in their billing infrastructure of out-of-pocket expenses.

Or how about the case of seventy-one-year-old Ian Wilson, the former chief executive officer of Aurora Foods, maker of Mrs. Butterworth's pancake syrup and Mrs. Paul's fish sticks.[4] He admitted to masking millions of dollars in promotional expenses by falsifying the company's financial statements to cover up for a failed marketing plan that brought in little revenue. When asked why such a bright and mature businessman and CEO of a publicly traded company would do such a thing, court documents revealed: "He did it to satisfy earnings-per-share expectations of Wall Street analysts and the expectations of Aurora investors." In that case, "right" (or "achievement") was determined by forward motion—meeting the earnings expectations of Wall Street, no matter what the cost—and "wrong" was anything that got in the way of Mr. Wilson accomplishing that goal.

The achievement mentality is accompanied by three main psychological rationalizations that set this alarming ethic in motion: excuses, apathy, and economic pressure.

Excuses

The first rationalization is to justify the corrupt behavior, or make excuses for the action. It says, "If my plan works, no one will get hurt, and everyone will be paid back. I will be happy with that outcome." This is a crucial point in terms of understanding the psychology of fraud.

This kind of mentality is simply known as avarice. Webster's dictionary defines *avarice* as "excessive or insatiable desire for wealth or gain." To the perpetrator, this first rationalization is seen as a "cure-all," or as referred to in the industry, "the cure," but its true name is "avarice" or "greed."

The best example I can give of "the cure" is my own case involving ZZZZ Best Carpet Cleaning. I (and my fraud team) instituted the "borrow from Peter to pay Paul" adage. The "cure" was my 6,000,000 shares of ZZZZ Best stock traded on the NASDAQ and free trading for years. The idea was to keep the company alive until then in order to pay off investors by the sale of stock. At that point, the lies could stop and the guilt would be swept away. In business, this is known as a "Ponzi scheme." In almost every Ponzi scheme, there is a "cure," or profitable deal, which will materialize and provide enough cash to pay off the investors. The investors are not thought of as *victims*. This allows the perpetrators to lie to investors and deceive the auditors free of guilt because the brilliant scheme includes paying everyone back.

In the end, my own rationalizations deceived me, and I paid for my mistakes.

Jim Donahue, the brilliant Stanford educated mathematician who managed a hedge fund that even lured federal judges, pleaded guilty to what prosecutors have called the biggest single securities fraud in U.S. history.[5] Donahue's cure for a down year was investing more than $90 million of the money he managed into United Airline options. His plan to recoup previous losses backfired when Iraq invaded Kuwait; gas prices suffered, and so did Donahue's highly speculative investment. To inform his investors that he lost all their money, he made a video and distributed it in the investment community.

Employee theft is on the rise for a similar justification called *entitlement*.[6] Someone who feels he is entitled to compensation might rationalize, "The company is profitable. They should have given me the raise. They didn't, and now I'm going to take what is rightfully mine."

Therefore, it is not hard to understand how the problem escalates over time. Months or even years later, those same people are now lying to Wall Street on 10Q's or 10K's or lying to banks (this time the loan is in the millions) or stealing bigger sums of money from the corporation that has so faithfully employed them. When achievement is the "new ethic" and the conscience is appeased by rationalization and entitlement arguments, *everything* is fair game.

If right equals forward motion and society judges success by accomplishments, then the compromises are worth the sacrifices. It begins as a temporary relaxation of ethics—everyone is doing it, and the "cure" will solve everything. No one will get hurt, and the promise of a future deal will make up for today's losses.

Apathy

The second rationalization is apathy, which believes, "Why not? Everyone else is doing it." This mentality is the infrastructure of what is known as the "right equals forward motion" ethic. Both corporate fraud perpetrators and average consumers can testify to the power of apathy.

Every day consumers are entrenched in the monotony of applying for credit cards, car loans, and second mortgages. They will often inflate their earnings on credit applications to qualify for the latest gas-guzzling SUV or the luxurious home one block closer to the beach. These average consumers will often justify their deceit by thinking, *I'm going to make the payments anyway...everyone does it.* Fraud has become a widespread "ethic epidemic" even among the average consumer!

A woman who owns a local floral shop kites a *few* checks to meet payroll. A retail owner manipulates just a *few* numbers on his inventory list. Movie houses send out just a *few* false reviews. It all starts with just a *few* compromises.

How else are average people compromising their character? Tax season. Thousands of people inflate their expenses and fail to disclose all income. Why? *Everyone* does it. Some consumers have gone as far as submitting fraudulent tax returns to support inflated incomes. In California, the situation has escalated to the point that many banks have created special forms that allow them to verify the validity of tax returns. Even the IRS is taking measures to help prevent the fraud problem among consumers. Originally intended to replace lost or stolen forms, Form 4506 created by the IRS is now being used as a tool to help prevent fraud. All it takes is this apathetic mind-set, and an ordinary person—like you or me—becomes a fraud perpetrator.

Economic pressure

The third rationalization is the combination of economic pressure and the fear of failure. Economic pressure can cause severe psychological trauma, triggering an average person to consider fraud as an alternative. A woman can't meet payroll for her local floral shop; the retail owner has suppliers clamoring for payment; or, the nursing home overcharges Medicare because too many beds remain empty.

A purchasing manager of a major airline company found himself in a financial predicament and started embezzling funds from the company. As a long-time employee, he had held various positions within the company. He and his wife had a financial goal to send their children to college, and now the oldest child had been accepted into an Ivy League university. Unable to fund this expensive college and, even less, save money to send the others to college, his pride compromised his integrity. He began to accept kickbacks from a vendor who had approached him with favors to get business. Burdened by guilt, he experienced severe stress as a result of his fraudulent activity, all of which began because he was too prideful to admit his financial inadequacy.

Here was an honest and dedicated professional who buckled when faced with economic pressure mixed with pride. He never would have considered compromising his principles during his first several years as a faithful employee.

> Pride goes before destruction, and a haughty spirit before a fall. Better to be of a humble spirit with the lowly, than to divide the spoil with the proud.
> —Proverbs 16:18–19

Another person also caved in to economic pressure. As senior vice president of a large California bank, he too was unable to bear the financial burden of his child's college tuition. It was never part of his career plan to lose his CPA license because of a white-collar crime.

The psychology of fraud finds its roots in the "right equals forward motion" ethic. In essence, the motives have been redefined. Ethical irresponsibility coupled with the "cure" and commonplace practice pave the way for fraudulent crime. Economic pressures that accompany achievement spell out the formula for financial disaster.

The sad reality of fraud is the anatomy of compromise:

- Contemplation (*I think I should do this because...*)

- Rationalization (*Everyone else does it; no one will get hurt.*)

- Consent (*I'm doing it guilt free!*)

Knowing the answer to "why" fraud is committed helps those responsible for due diligence to recognize that it can be *anyone*. If we learn to identify the warning signs, it may prove beneficial not only for those who may find themselves in a similar situation, but also for us.

Good will come to him who is generous and lends freely, who conducts his affairs with justice.

—PSALM 112:5, NIV

CHAPTER 4

Business Ethics *Is* a Religious Issue

In this post-Enron era, the "ethics" industry is flourishing. Prior to this time there was limited discussion and understanding of the scope and definition of this "hot" topic. It's unfortunate that it took the financial ruin of several large public companies for lawmakers to realize that values and integrity *do* play a major role in the corporate world.

It is very important to drill down into the subject of ethics. We see a host of "Ethics Training" consulting programs stirred up by the Sarbanes-Oxley Act (SOX). While I realize that not everyone will agree with me, I strongly believe that business ethics must be built around the Protestant/Christian ethic, sometimes referred to as Judeo-Christian ethic.

With the introduction of SOX Section 404, all publicly traded companies must evaluate their internal control environment in 2004 or 2005 (depending on the market capitalization and when the fiscal year ends for their company). This includes an assessment of the ethics and morals of corporate management! We will discuss SOX in greater detail in chapter five, under the section entitled "What Is the Sarbanes-Oxley Act?"

Integrity and Ethical Values

My experience has been that men and women who make a sincere attempt to follow God's rules and a biblical approach to business ethics experience positive benefits. Business people with godly ethics experience a certain calmness in their lives, because God is protecting them from the onslaught of evil. Over time, God honors them financially because of their commitment to a higher standard of values and morals. Their children, if they have any, learn to respect them and carry on their tradition for godly living. Most of the people in this group are active in one or more faith-based ministries. Often times they are the ones who stand alone in a group when tough decisions have to be made. Consequently, they may experience periods of loneliness while holding to their ethical positions, but God ultimately honors them. They are enterprising people who are frugal in their business and personal lives but generous and compassionate to the plight of others. Their faces radiate the inner peace that exists in their lives.

Dr. Kurt Senske writes in his book *Executive Values: A Christian Approach to Organizational Leadership*:

> The Golden Rule of Leadership is not a new concept. It is an old concept, at least as old as the Christian tradition, and business leaders have tried to apply it to business practice before. In seventeenth-century England, for example, *caveat emptor* was the order of the day, cautioning buyers against untrustworthy merchants. In that same century, George Fox, founder of the Society of Friends (Quakers), encouraged a new business ethic based on truthfulness, dependability, and fixed prices. For Fox, this was the only logical outcome of practicing one's faith in the world of business. Quaker businessmen heeded his call, quickly became perceived as some of the few people who could be trusted, and became extremely successful. Their success forced other businessmen to adopt the Quaker ethical model in order to survive in the marketplace. Imagine the radical leap of faith these Quakers initially had to take in order to bring about such significant changes in the business world.[1]

Management must convey the message that integrity and ethical values cannot be compromised, and employees must receive and understand the message. It is up to management to continually demonstrate, through words and actions, a commitment to high ethical standards.

Begin by implementing a code of conduct and other internal policies regarding acceptable business practice and expected standards of ethical and moral behavior for the company.

For example, consider whether:

- Codes are comprehensive, addressing conflicts of interest, illegal or other improper payments, anti-competitive guidelines, inside trading.

- All employees acknowledge said codes periodically.

- Employees understand what behavior is acceptable or unacceptable, and know what to do if they encounter improper behavior.

- If a written code of conduct does not exist, the management culture emphasizes the importance of integrity and ethical behavior. This may be communicated orally in staff meetings, in one-on-one interface, or by example when dealing with day-to-day activities.

- Establishment of the "Tone at the Top"—including explicit moral guidance about what is right and wrong—and extent of its communication throughout the organization.

For example:

- Is the management's commitment to integrity and ethics communicated effectively throughout the enterprise, both in words and deeds?

- Are employees getting the message to do the right thing or to cut corners to make a "quick buck"?

- Does management deal appropriately when there are signs that problems exist (e.g., potential defective products or hazardous wastes, especially when the cost of identifying problems and dealing with the issues could be large)?

- Does management display the "do as I say, not as I do" mentality when dealing with employees, suppliers, customers, investors, creditors, insurers, competitors, and auditors?

In other words, is management conducting business on a high ethical stance and insisting the rest of the company do the same, or does management pay little attention to ethical standards? The following are examples of the types of procedures management should have in place:

- Everyday dealings with customers, suppliers, employees, and other parties are based on honesty and fairness (e.g., customer's over-payment or a supplier's under-billing are not ignored; no efforts are made to find a way to reject an employee's legitimate claim for benefits; and reports to lenders are complete, accurate, and not misleading).

- Appropriateness of remedial action taken in response to departures from approved policies and procedures or violations of the code of conduct; the extent to which remedial action is clearly communicated throughout the entity.

If management responds to violations of behavioral standards, and disciplinary actions are taken as a result of those violations, then employees know they will suffer the consequences for violating those standards.

Another area is management's attitude toward intervention or overriding established controls. Documentation and appropriate explanations are essential in communicating management's policy regarding intervention. It is imperative that a manager, or any representative or officer of the company, does *not* override established standards. This is totally unacceptable and prohibited behavior. Any deviations from established policies should be investigated and well documented.

Some of the catalysts for such deviations may result from the following:

- Pressure to meet unrealistic performance targets—particularly for short-term results—and to the extent to which compensation is based on achieving those performance targets.

- Conditions such as extreme incentives or temptations exist that can unnecessarily and unfairly test people's adherence to ethical values.

- Compensation and promotions based solely on achievement of short-term performance targets.

- Controls not in place to reduce temptations that might otherwise exist.

Business Ethics Begins in Business Schools

The business press has commented that many of the top business schools have been revising and overhauling their programs dramatically. On September 17, 2003, the *Wall Street Journal* noted:

In the post-Enron era, MBA programs—Harvard in particular—have come in for some caustic criticism for producing graduates obsessed with making money regardless of the ethical consequences. To some people, MBA graduates are at the root of all the corporate greed and dishonesty. In a public-opinion survey about how companies can mend their reputations, one respondent declared, "Get rid of the Harvard MBAs." After all, two infamous Enron executives—former Chief Executive Jeffrey Skilling and former Chief Financial Officer Andrew Fastow—hold MBA degrees from Harvard and Northwestern University's Kellogg School of Management, respectively.

Even President George W. Bush, a Harvard MBA graduate, has publicly urged business schools to "be principled teachers of right and wrong and not surrender to moral confusion and relativism." Business schools got the message. They are busy infusing more ethics training than ever before into their curricula, as well as trying to screen applications for integrity before admitting students into the graduate program. The article continues:

In fact, some schools are doing background checks to verify the accuracy of applications, while Harvard added an essay question to its applications requiring people to explain how they handled an ethical dilemma. "We hope through our admissions process to attract students with a strong upbringing," says Prof. Paine. "We are preparing young people for their role in life and building what came before."

Recently, AACSB International, the major business-school accrediting organization, increased the emphasis on ethics in the standards that business schools must meet to receive accreditation. "Before

Enron, ethics didn't occupy a central role at many schools," says Carolyn Woo, chairman of AACSB and dean of the Mendoza College of Business at the University of Notre Dame. "We must challenge students about how much their values are worth and develop an awareness in them of the ethical implications of business decisions. They must have their antennae up and not be naïve."[2]

On August 16, 2002, the *Associated Press State and Local Wire* also noted that:

Posters hanging around the University of Akron business school urge students to enroll in a new philosophy department course on business ethics. "The students are suddenly interested in businesses' ethics," said Stephen Hallam, dean of Akron's College of Business Administration. "It used to be if you said 'business ethics' students would roll their eyes. Now it's the hottest topic going." Hallam said that in the wake of accounting scandals that have destroyed some of the nation's largest companies, nearly all of the school's faculty members are revising their courses to make sure they are including case studies about business ethics.[3]

The story is the same at business schools across the country; they are scrambling to beef up the ethics components of their coursework, responding to the upsurge in interest among students as well as the prodding of lawmakers.

On September 25, 2003, *SmartPros* reported that incoming MBA students at the University of California, Davis partook in a mandatory "ethics boot camp" prior to starting fall classes. The program required 150 students entering the Graduate School of Management to complete selected readings in ethics and submit an essay about how they resolved a difficult ethical dilemma. They then attended a session that discussed leadership, values, and individual corporate responsibility, focusing on a case study about providing assistance to a dying man they encounter in the mountains.

> "Business is increasingly complex," said Dean Nicole Woolsey Biggart, who established the program. "Students who are well meaning and honest need guidance in navigating what can be ethically complex situations."[4]

But it takes more than upgrades to the MBA program to effect long-term change and reformation. Changes in the "old school" of thought must take place as well. Reformation of business practices also begins with today's corporate directors.

"One Nation Under God"

Changing the programs of business schools and sending directors to ethics seminars is a superficial solution to the problem. Our nation's morality problems stem from a spirit of "Antichrist(ian)" that permeates our society. Any mention of the names "God" or "Jesus" agitates some Americans.

What this group of people fails to realize is that separation of church and state was never the goal of our Founding Fathers as it has come into being today. "First Amendment rights," as so many use in loose terms, have become watered down through time. A commonly known fact is that early American settlers came here to *escape* religious persecution and to be able to practice their religion freely. The First Amendment was created to guarantee every citizen the right to worship without the federal government interfering in that worship or establishing a national church, such as the one in England. In other words:

> It meant that men could be as religious as they wanted to be and that even states could be distinctly

Christian in their laws, but that the federal government was forbidden to intrude....When the
Supreme Court adopted language Thomas Jefferson
had used in a private letter and began making
rulings in terms of a "wall of separation between
church and state," the break from original intent
was complete.[5]

Michael S. Heath, in his commentary in the *Maine Sunday
Telegram,* underscores the point:

Whether it is taking God out of the Pledge of
Allegiance or removing the Ten Commandments
from a courthouse in Alabama, a campaign is under way to eliminate religion from government.
Many have already formed an opinion about the
nature of this campaign. Some see it as an attempt
to undermine the Judeo-Christian foundations of
our culture.[6]

Yet on closer reflection, it is clear that the effort to remove religious symbols from our public life represents a dangerous departure
from the heritage of a free people.

Where did this heritage begin? Many say the Founding Fathers.
Others say the Magna Carta. The correct answer is found in a book
much maligned by the opponents of religion—the Bible.

The Founding Fathers knew the Bible well. In it they discovered
the true source of man's freedom. Proclaiming liberty is a concept
that is rooted in the Word of God. The prophet Jeremiah spoke of
liberty on the captivity of Israel in Babylon. "Then you recently
turned and did what was right in My sight—every man proclaiming
liberty to his neighbor" (Jer. 34:15). It is, in fact, the Bible that first
taught man his duty to "proclaim liberty to his neighbor."

One of America's most precious treasures is Thomas Jefferson's
first draft of the Declaration of Independence. Congress insisted on

adding the phrase "endowed by their Creator with certain inalienable rights" as a precursor to his original words. Those who were instrumental in laying the foundation for our government were careful to state in unmistakable terms that the rights of mankind derive not from any parliament or kings but from their Creator!

We must first acknowledge that business ethics must be founded based upon a religious model that teaches us right from wrong. We have long been viewed as a nation with its roots in a historic Protestant Christian (Judeo-Christian) culture, and I strongly urge that we should look to the Bible as our basis for making such decisions. The key elements of this ethics model are:

1. *Stewardship:* Responsible care over the assets and lives of employees entrusted to the senior management and board of directors of a company

2. *Justice:* Accountability and fairness in all financial and employee matters

3. *Charity:* Displays of corporate compassion to those in need

4. *Accountability:* Subject to the review by others

5. *Morals:* Following a biblical model of standards

The Reformation of Corporate America needs to be a Bible-based reformation. It is more than following the "Golden Rule" as some would suggest. It is a detailed study and application of Bible concepts, and there are hundreds of such concepts to guide our thinking. This approach will yield good decision making and help stop the periodic cycles of fraud and government intervention we have seen for almost a century in our nation. This is the key in preserving our constitutional republic.

Perhaps you don't know where to begin. I've compiled a series of checklists to aid you in such decision making for various levels in the corporate environment in Appendix II. These are merely to guide you and give you a foundation upon which to build your own decision-making checklists.

The next chapter will provide an in-depth look at the Sarbanes-Oxley Act of 2002 and how you can prepare your company to meet the new compliance standards.

To reform a world, to reform a nation, no wise man will undertake; and all but foolish men know, that the only solid, though a far slower reformation, is what each begins and perfects on himself.[1]
—Thomas Carlyle (1795–1881),
Scottish essayist, historian.
"Signs of the Times" (1829) first published in *Edinburgh Review*, no. 98.

CHAPTER 5

Reformation of Corporate America

When we think of the word *reformation*, we usually attribute it to change in the political or religious climate. Our country's history reflects that we are a nation constantly evolving and searching for a better quality of life for all its inhabitants. Reformation is coming to America again, but it is a reformation unlike any other we have seen in the history of this great country.

When President George W. Bush signed the Sarbanes-Oxley Act (SOX) into effect in 2002, it was an effort on the government's part to enforce tighter penalties on corporate executives who broke the law. The SOX Act, however, cannot change people's work ethics. For integrity and ethics to improve in the corporate world, people must be willing to change.

As I stated earlier, one of the most frequent questions clients ask me is: "What can we do to keep this from occurring again?" My reply to them is simple. The SOX Act is the federal government's attempt to legislate morality. True integrity is an issue of the heart and reaches beyond the governing law.

Effectively, SOX with the COSO (Committee of Sponsoring Organizations of the Treadway Commission) model requires an independent analysis and testing of the ethics control environment in Corporate America. This raises a number of interesting questions:

1. What is the definition of integrity and ethics?

2. Who is qualified to evaluate this in the corporate environment?

3. What is the basis for defining what is right and wrong?

4. Who should be providing the training for these evaluations?

5. How do we communicate ethics effectively?

6. How much is it going to cost us?

To help answer these, let's first look at the history of Corporate America over the last seventy-five years. The following significant business milestones set forth a striking example of the volatile and cyclical nature of ethics in the United States.

- Stock Market Crash of 1929

- Securities and Exchange Commission (SEC)—established in the 1930s

- Period of economic stability in the 1950s– 1960s

- Sharp rise in financial fraud, illegal corporate acts, bribes, political payoffs, and kickbacks— 1970s

- Foreign Corrupt Practices Act (enacted 1972)

- The Cohen Commission (installed 1977– 1978)

- AICPA—SEC Practice Section established (1977)

- The 1980s and 1990s—era of rapid growth

- Tort Reform 1996

- Rapid rise in wealth/greed—1980s–1990s

- COSO established in 1992–1994, but ignored by many

- Enron collapses; Arthur Andersen fails— 2001

- SOX and the PCAOB established—2002

- Accounting scandals 2001–2004

The rise and fall of periods of strong ethics and stability often follow the rise of corruption and rampant fraud in the United States. Somehow we need to find a real solution!

What Is Sarbanes-Oxley?

In the face of accounting scandals and fraudulent business and accounting practices, a new era of internal control reviews has emerged. The Sarbanes-Oxley Act (SOX), Section 404—Management's Assessment of Internal Controls—requires all public companies to assess their internal control environment.

In July 2002 President Bush signed into law the Sarbanes-Oxley Bill (SOX). (See Appendix I for a summary of the act.) This legislation is becoming one of the most far-reaching congressional acts in recent history.

SOX is the "price you pay" in a constitutional republic and free enterprise system when you ignore the Judeo-Christian faith-based business ethics needed to keep the financial records in accordance with GAAP.

Under the new SOX regulations, CEOs and CFOs of reporting companies are required to submit certifications regarding the effectiveness of the company's internal control systems to the SEC starting in late 2004 or 2005, depending on market capitalization and fiscal year ends. The SEC defines disclosure controls as those procedures that are designed to ensure that information required to be disclosed by the company in Exchange Act reports is accumulated and communicated to the company's management, including the CFO and CEO, to allow timely decisions regarding required disclosure. The SEC recently issued guidelines specifying that the Internal Control Framework published by COSO (the Committee of Sponsoring Organizations of the Treadway Commission) is to be used to evaluate the internal control systems of reporting companies.

SOX is an interesting blend of federally mandated disclosures and controls that are clinical in nature but require the teaching of morals and ethics in the workplace via the COSO model. It is my firm belief that good business ethics are not simply the corporate governance committee meeting eight times a year or the audit committee completing a ten-page checklist. Rather it is faith speaking to the heart and conscience of man.

The COSO Internal Control Framework

COSO stands for "Committee of Sponsoring Organizations" and is a voluntary private-sector organization dedicated to improving the quality of financial reporting through business ethics, effective internal controls, and corporate governance. The committee was formed in 1985 to sponsor the National Commission on Fraudulent Financial Reporting, also known as the Treadway Commission. The commission studied the causal factors that can lead to fraudulent financial reporting and developed recommendations for public companies and their independent auditors, as well as for the SEC and other regulators.

COSO developed and published a recommended methodology, illustrated by the graphic on the next page, for evaluating the effectiveness of a company's internal control systems and procedures.

The Securities and Exchange Commission now requires that the COSO model for this SOX evaluation be used. The COSO model was developed by a blue ribbon task force in 1992 and has been catapulted into the limelight as the "gold standard" for such evaluations. So now we have a very interesting situation in that COSO's evaluation tools require a thorough review of integrity and ethical values of all public companies.

THE COSO INTERNAL CONTROL FRAMEWORK

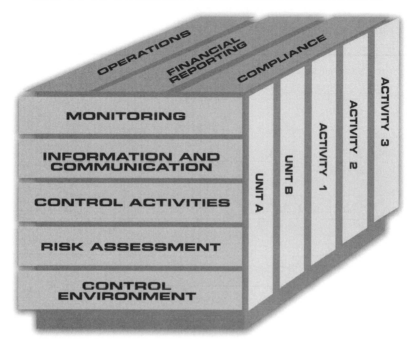

This graphic illustrates the interrelation between the five components of internal control with the three main objective areas of operations, financial reporting, and compliance with applicable laws and regulations. It also illustrates that the review process is to be applied to the entire organization on both the entity and activity levels to provide management with criteria by which to evaluate the internal controls.

The five components of the COSO Internal Control Framework/ Compliance matrix are:

1. Control environment

2. Risk assessment

3. Control activities

4. Information and communication

5. Monitoring

Control environment

The control environment provides an atmosphere in which people conduct their activities and carry out their control responsibilities. It serves as the foundation for the other components. Within this environment, management assesses risk to the achievement of specified objectives. Control activities are implemented to help ensure that the management directives to address the risks are carried out. Meanwhile, relevant information is captured and communicated throughout the organization. The entire process is monitored and modified as conditions warrant.

PHASE I	PHASE II	PHASE III	PHASE IV	PHASE V
Overview of Control Environment & Documentation	Risk Assessment and Controls Review	Evaluation Design and Implementation of Tests/ Solutions for the Organization	Testing Controls and Monitoring	Issue Internal Control Report Meetings With Auditors and Audit Committee

As previously mentioned, the control environment sets the tone of an organization, i.e., the "Tone at the Top," influencing the control mind-set of its individuals. This is the cornerstone for all of the internal control components, providing discipline and structure. Our approach identifies, formulates, and evaluates the following components of the control environment in terms of the financial, operational, and compliance objectives of the company:

- Integrity, ethical values

- Commitment to competence

- Board of directors and audit committee involvement

- Management's philosophy and operating style

- Organizational structure

- Assignment and linking of authority and responsibility

- HR policies and practices

Risk assessment

The risk assessment component of internal control first requires an analysis of the operational, financial, and compliance objectives of the company. The process of identifying and analyzing risk is an iterative process that is critical to the success of the internal control system. Management should identify and prioritize risks at all levels of an entity or activity. Management should also identify the processes in place that are intended to manage them. The analysis of risk assessment includes the following elements tailored to the specific requirements of the company:

- Evaluation of objectives

- Financial reporting risk

- Risk identification procedures

- Risk analysis

- Circumstances requiring special attention

- Mechanisms to identify change

Control activities

Control activities are the company's policies and procedures that are put in place to carry out management directives. Effective control activities are designed to ensure that necessary actions are taken to address and manage risks in order to achieve the entity's objectives. Control activities occur throughout the organization, at all levels and in all functions. They include a range of activities as diverse as approvals, authorizations, verifications, reconciliations, reviews of operating performance, security of assets, and the segregation of duties. Our analysis will focus on the following activities across organizational, entity, and activity levels of control:

- Top level reviews

- Direct functional or activity management

- Information processing

- Physical controls

- Performance indicators

- Segregation of duties

- Policies and procedures

Information and communication

Information systems produce reports that contain operational, financial, and compliance-related information and support running and controlling the business. They deal not only with internally generated data, but also information about external events, activities, and conditions necessary for informed business decision making and external reporting. Effective communication also must occur in a broader sense, flowing down, across, and up the organization.

All personnel must receive a clear message from top management that control responsibilities must be taken seriously. They must understand their own roles in the internal control system, as well as how individual activities relate to the work of others. They must also have a method of communicating information upstream to management. Finally, there also needs to be effective communication with external parties, such as customers, suppliers, regulators, and shareholders.

Management should analyze, document, and recommend changes to the company's information and communication systems along the following dimensions:

- Information quality

- Appropriate content

- Timely

- Current

- Accurate

- Accessible

- Communication—down, across, and up

- Internal

- External

Monitoring

Monitoring is accomplished through a combination of ongoing review activities and separate evaluations. Ongoing monitoring occurs in the course of operations and includes regular management and supervisory activities and the actions that other personnel take in performing their duties. The scope and frequency of separate evaluations will depend primarily on an assessment of risks and the effectiveness of ongoing monitoring procedures. Internal control deficiencies should be reported upstream, with serious matters reported to top management and the board audit committee.

When reporting, it is important to keep in mind the following issues:

- The process should assess the internal control system's performance over time.

- Consider the evaluation process and methodology.

- When reporting deficiencies, remember to:

    —Explain what occurred.

—Say to whom it is addressed.

—Include proper documentation.

—Give a corrective action plan.

While much of SOX is applicable to publicly traded companies, there are ten sections that are also applicable to private companies as follows:

1. Section 306—Thirty days minimum notice for pension plan changes

2. Section 307—Pension blackouts

3. Section 802—Criminalization of document alteration

4. Section 803—Non-dischargeability in bankruptcy of debts flowing from securities violations

5. Section 902—Attempts and conspiracies to commit fraud

6. Section 903—Enhanced penalties for committing mail or wire fraud

7. Section 904—Enhanced penalties for Erisa violations

8. Section 1001 (Recommendation only)— CEO must certify corporate tax return

9. Section 1102—Criminalization of tampering with or impeding an official proceeding

10. Section 1107—Criminalization of retaliation against whistleblower

COSO, however, is not sitting still, waiting for someone to take initiative in implementing these components. A new framework, Enterprise Risk Management (ERM), has been developed for possible adoption in 2005. This new framework builds off of the old one but adds three new components:

1. Objective setting

2. Event identification

3. Risk recognition

This new model is highly risk-focused, and I believe we will continue to see improvements to the COSO model for years to come.

The Long Arm of the Law

The SOX Act is far reaching, which is good because the problem is not isolated to public companies. In addition to the focus on Section 404, Internal Controls, it should be noted that sweeping changes in the following areas have also occurred:

- Audit committee leadership/financial experts

- Audit partner rotation

- Record retention

- Enhanced GAAP disclosures

- Criminal penalties for defrauding shareholders of publicly traded companies

- Increased criminal penalties under the Securities Exchange Act of 1934

As Corporate America wrestles with SOX, several different groups have vested interests:

- The registrants' independent accounting firms

- Consultants that assist the registrant with implementation of Section 404 of SOX

- The Securities and Exchange Commission

- The PCAOB

Certain key SOX Section 404 implementation issues relating to the initial adoption are surfacing such as those identified in the December 2003 AICPA National Conference on Current SEC Developments in Washington, where representatives of PricewaterhouseCoopers noted the following implementation issues:

1. **Implementation Issue: Significant Effort by Management**

   - Substantial effort for both management and the external auditor

     - Does management have the necessary resources?

     - "The more you know, the bigger it gets."

     - "The more you know, the less controls you have."

     - Rotation of testing is not permitted.

2. **Implementation Issues: Related to the Issuer**

   - Documentation of controls

     - Depth and breadth of the documentation process

     - How much is enough?

- Extent of testing of operating effectiveness

  - Coverage

  - Sample sizes

  - Who can perform the testing?

3. **Implementation Issues: Application of Proposed Standards**

   - Multiple locations or business units

     - Applicable to the auditor as well as the company

     - What is the meaning of "large portion" of a company's operations and financial position?

     - How do you handle the situation where all locations or business units are of equal size?

   - Service organizations—SAS No. 70 reporting

     - Controls over the initiation, recording, processing, and reporting at the service organization are part of the company's assessment

     - Need to take an inventory early to identify these situations

     - What if the SAS No. 70 auditor is the same as the external auditor of the company?

     - Dating of report

- ▪ Application in foreign countries
- Safeguarding of assets
  - ▪ Definition of internal controls: "Provides reasonable assurance regarding prevention or timely detection of unauthorized acquisition, use, or disposition of the company's assets that could have material effect on the financial statements."
  - ▪ What are the boundaries of safeguarding of assets as it relates to internal control over financial reporting? Areas to consider:
    - —Retail inventory shrinkage
    - —Music piracy
    - —Disaster recovery
    - —Insurance underwriting
- Acquisitions close to fiscal year end
  - ▪ Significant acquisitions made close to year end are included in assessment.
  - ▪ How do you get satisfied with the acquired control environment?
  - ▪ Is a scope limitation permitted?
- Using the work of others
  - ▪ How should the auditor determine whether he or she has achieved the "principle evidence"?

- What is the meaning of "limited" regarding procedures in areas where use of the work of others should be limited?

- Walkthroughs

    - The auditor "should trace all types of transactions and events both recurring and unusual."

    - Could encompass hundreds of transactions and events that are not material.

- Sampling

    - Testing size/extent of testing

    - How much is appropriate?

- Communication of internal control deficiencies

    - Requires auditor to communicate all internal control deficiencies to management, including those identified by management, internal auditors, and others

    - In a large multinational company, this could result in the reporting of hundreds of internal control deficiencies.

Only time will tell the effectiveness of this piece of legislation. It certainly has provided more reason for caution than prior to the SOX Act. As the quote by Thomas Carlyle eloquently states, "... a far slower reformation is what each begins and perfects in himself." You can't legislate morality; it must come from changed hearts.

It is this mental metamorphosis that we must grasp. We must think and act differently to effect change. There is no "wink and nod" in this reformation. The bridge to a new reformed future will crumble if we don't take this seriously.

Is there anyone here who, planning to build a new house, doesn't first sit down and figure the cost so you'll know if you can complete it? If you only get the foundation laid and then run out of money, you're going to look pretty foolish. Everyone passing by will poke fun at you: "He started something he couldn't finish."

—LUKE 14:28–30, THE MESSAGE

CHAPTER 6

Ancient Foundational Principles for Today's Business Environment

One of the great blessings of a public accounting vocation is the opportunity to see the "insides" of hundreds of businesses and to look deep into their financial structures and organizational designs. During my years as a CPA, I have also spent thousands of hours volunteering in various faith-based organizations, particularly as the treasurer of churches and Christian schools.

Over time, I have noted some interesting parallels to the so-called business world and religious environments. Good businesses and good Christian ministries have certain common characteristics:

- Accountability at the top

- Healthy respect for internal accounting controls

- Respect for the customers/people

- Care for employees

- Limited debt/leverage ratios

- Desire to be profitable, but not at the expense of gouging the customer

- Respect for God's day of rest: Sunday

- Strong ethics throughout the organization

- Appropriate discipline for unacceptable behavior

- Respect for God's authority

As I reflect on these common characteristics, I have concluded that successful businesses, as a whole, pattern themselves after certain biblical concepts and guidelines. Let's look at three areas in particular: corporate structure, code of conduct, and corporate oversight.

CORPORATE STRUCTURE	
Church Government	Corporate Government
Elder boards	Board of directors
Deacons	Senior management

CODES OF CONDUCT	
Church Government	Corporate Government
Biblical standards	Corporate code of ethics
Disciplinary actions	Disciplinary committees

CORPORATE OVERSIGHT	
Church Government	Corporate Government
Church hierarchy	Audit committees
Denominational oversight	Internal audit departments

Elder Boards and Corporate Boards of Directors

Many mainstream churches in America pattern the selection of their board of elders based upon this passage:

> It is a true saying that if someone wants to be an elder, he desires an honorable responsibility. For an elder must be a man whose life cannot be spoken against. He must be faithful to his wife. He must exhibit self-control, live wisely, and have a good repu-

tation. He must enjoy having guests in his home
and must be able to teach. He must not be a heavy
drinker or be violent. He must be gentle, peace lov-
ing, and not one who loves money. He must manage his own family well, with children who respect
and obey him. For if a man cannot manage his own
household, how can he take care of God's church?
An elder must not be a new Christian, because he
might be proud of being chosen so soon, and the
Devil will use that pride to make him fall.

—1 Timothy 3:1–6, nlt

The church's board of elders usually addresses issues such as
doctrine, church policy, senior elder accountability, financial health
of the church, and any other strategic issues. Corporate boards,
however, address issues such as corporate policies, strategic decisions,
CEO accountability, capital requirements, and so on.

Although the ultimate goal varies, perhaps corporate boards
could follow suit and establish similar guidelines when selecting their
board members. In doing so, they would establish the "Tone at the
Top" and foster higher ethical standards.

Deacon Boards and Senior Management

Senior management of a company addresses sales, R&D, finan-
cial/accounting matters, human resources, and capital expenditures.
Deacon boards address the status of the physical facility, operation of
the services, and accounting and treasury functions.

In the same way, deacons must be people who are
respected and have integrity. They must not be
heavy drinkers and must not be greedy for money.
They must be committed to the revealed truths of
the Christian faith and must live with a clear conscience.

—1 Timothy 3:8–9, nlt

Church Discipline vs.
Government/Corporate Discipline

Churches are given biblical guidelines for governance. (See Romans 13.) The government also provides oversight and discipline in addition to the governance provided by corporate oversight. This was particularly clear in the months after the collapse of Enron.

The SEC's Enforcement Division has been extremely active in recent years in the issuance of reports known as Accounting and Auditing Enforcement Releases (AAERs). The AAERs address these accounting and auditing failures. AAERs are serious matters issued as a result of in-depth SEC violations and have been on the rise at an alarming rate. A historical perspective showing the increase in such punitive public announcements is remarkable.

YEARS	NO. OF ISSUED AAERS
1998/1999	102
1999/2000	139
2000/2001	131
2001/2002	176
2002/2003	245

According to the chart, there has been a 150 percent increase of accounting failures/fraudulent activity in the last five years, which is indicative of the rapid rate of misdeeds and corruption in Corporate America. This further underscores the need for a dramatic overhaul and reformation in the corporate environment.

Some of the recent notable SEC enforcement actions are as follows:

AAER NO.	DATE	IDENTIFIED MATTER
1640	10/2/02	Andrew S. Fastow, CFO, Enron Corporation
ISSUES:		Revenue recognition, sham sales, backdating documents

AAER NO.	DATE	IDENTIFIED MATTER
1642	10/07/02	**Buford Yates, WorldCom, Director of Accounting of WorldCom, Inc.**
ISSUES:	Capitalized costs	
1650	10/10/02	**Betty L. Vinson and Troy M. Normal, accountants in the general accounting department of WorldCom, Inc.**
ISSUES:	Capitalized costs	
1661	11/13/02	**Ernst & Young**
ISSUES:	Alleged violation of auditor independence of the financial statements of PeopleSoft, Inc. 1994–2000	
1663	11/14/02	**Albert Dunlop, former chairman and CEO of Sunbeam, et al.**
ISSUES:	GAAP violations, nondisclosure of transactions	
1673	11/25/02	**Ilse Cappel, CPA, Senior Treasurer/ Manager at Peregrine Systems Inc.**
ISSUES:	Revenue recognition, fraudulent accounts receivable, insider trading	
1709	1/29/03	**KPMG, LLP, Joseph T. Boyle, Michael A. Conway, Anthony Polanski, and Randell A. Sarfran, partners with various roles on the Xerox Engagement 1998–1999**
ISSUES:	Equipment leases, revenue recognition	
1744	3/20/02	**HealthSouth Corporation and Richard M. Scrushy**
1759	4/16/03	**Matthew C. Gless, former CFO of Peregrine Systems Inc.**
ISSUES:	Revenue recognition, side letter agreements	

AAER NO.	DATE	IDENTIFIED MATTER
1787	5/22/03	**PricewaterhouseCoopers, LLP, SmarTalk,**
ISSUES:	Revenue recognition, altering workpapers	
1821	7/28/03	**Citigroup, Inc.**
ISSUES:	Alleged assistance with two Houston-based corporations, Enron and Dynergy, to enhance their financial presentations through complex structured transactions	
1881	9/30/03	**Scott Millen, CPA, Chief Accountant and Senior VP Finance for PurchasePro, Inc.**
ISSUES:	Revenue recognition, nonperformance contract	

The post-Enron era is begging for "order out of chaos" and the need for standards of conduct.

God's Word is the only authority that will drive a nation into sound decision making. It is a road map, if you will, to reformation in business ethics. The Bible brings wisdom into our hearts and minds. Through salvation in Christ we look at events differently because the Holy Spirit resides within us and convicts us when we sin. There are hundreds of Bible verses that address business matters, some of which I have quoted earlier in the book. The Judeo-Christian faith has a track record that strongly suggests it is the only viable answer.

Chris Seay, in his book *The Tao of Enron*, writes:

> Media reports continue to paint an ugly portrait of an entire corporate culture built on rapacious greed. With zero regards for how their aggressively self-obsessed and often immoral actions would bankrupt the retirement and investment portfolios of thousands of investors (and put thousands of then-unknowing employees out of work), key

executives at Enron enriched themselves through complicated series of sham corporations and highly suspect accounting procedures. What happened at Enron leads us to question our own trust in humanity and our expectations of the future.

Yet I am convinced that 99.9 percent of Enron employees are basically honest and fine people—and I include the former chairman in that group, despite the late-night comedians who have found in this corporate implosion a fresh source of material. Jay Leno joked, "This past Sunday, former Enron CEO Ken Lay went to a church in Houston. On the way out, a reporter asked him how he thought it was going to work out. Lay said, 'With God's help we'll get through it.' To which the devil said, 'Hey, I thought we had a deal.'"[1]

The Bible has been around a long time. It has served as a guide for living for generations of human civilizations. Why should it not also serve as the underpinnings of the Corporate Reformation in America? The need for integrity begins with a change of the heart, but for integrity to have a lasting impact, we need to begin teaching integrity at home.

Train up a child in the way he should go, and when he is old he will not depart from it.

—PROVERBS 22:6

CHAPTER 7

Integrity at Home:
Training Future Business Leaders
by Mary A. Steelman

In order for us to build a bridge to a future that represents an era
of integrity and godly ethics, we need to look at ethics training in
four areas:

1. Training at home

2. Training in the schools

3. Training in the churches

4. Training in the workplace

These four components are linked and form a continuum that
helps ensure a Reformation in Corporate America.

Ethics training, however, begins in the home. Parents have the
God-given responsibility to guide and instruct their children—the
future business leaders of our nation. It is important to fully understand how integrity and a personal code of ethics are conceived in the
home long before our sons and daughters enter the professional world.
Paul David Tripp, in his book *Age of Opportunity*, makes the following
statement: "The family is God's primary learning community."[1]

Parents desire to see their children lead successful and prosperous
lives and should employ every resource available to insure the well-
being and integrity of their children. Our society generally does not
encourage the values necessary to produce honesty and uprightness

in our children but, on the contrary, idolizes those who have "beat the system" and succeeded at their own expense.

As noted in the *Wall Street Journal* in March 2004, Martha Stewart was convicted on four counts related to the sale of her ImClone shares and related subsequent events.[2] She had the choice to accept or refuse the ImClone insider trading information, and she had a choice on how to properly communicate her activities to the federal authorities. "Choose a good reputation over great riches, for being held in high esteem is better than having silver or gold" (Prov. 22:1, NLT).

Where do we go to find appropriate foundational truths that lay the grid work of ethics and morals? How can we purposefully and systematically train our children and ourselves to do the right thing even when it hurts? Joyce Meyer, Christian speaker and author, stated in one of her teachings on integrity, "True integrity is doing the right thing even when no one else is looking." Isn't that what we want in our children and ourselves? Parents and guardians have a tremendous responsibility to teach moral principles and values to their children of all ages, and those principles should be based on timeless truths that have guided many to success. This means people must invest the time and energy to make this happen.

As part of the reformation needed in Corporate America, we must understand the foundation for business ethics begins early, continues to expand through the education cycle of the child, and is maintained and expanded by "continuing education" at the church and in the corporate environment. For those who hold to the Judeo-Christian faith, such ethics are found throughout the Bible, particularly in the Psalms and Proverbs. The implementation of these teachings along with other training tools will lay the groundwork for integrity in the home and the lives of our children. "Teach your children to choose the right path, and when they are older, they will remain upon it" (Prov. 22:6, NLT). "This promise is the scriptural expression of the principle on which all education rests; that a child's training influences what his later life will become. Without faith in this principle there would be no reason to educate in the home."[3] This is a wonderful promise given to parents, but it carries with it the responsibility to take the time to teach and train the children entrusted to our care.

This truly is the age of opportunity to win the battle for the hearts of our children because the heart is the soil in which the seeds of truth, honesty, and honor are planted. Seeds in the heart can be likened to a farmer who plants seeds in the ground and waits for them to mature. He plants...cultivates...waters...protects and finally reaps a superb harvest. Parents are planters and have the wonderful opportunity to sow into their children a sense of identity and destiny based on a genuine code of ethics. This planting places a hedge of knowledge and protection that will, over time, reap a harvest of integrity and virtue. It is this hedge that will often protect the businessperson, later in life, at those very critical moments when, faced with tough choices, they must ask, "What is the right thing to do?"

We live in a visually stimulated culture that inundates our children with information to discourage honesty and virtue. If a child does not have a foundation of values and beliefs, it will be difficult for them to discern right from wrong. In his book *Kingdom Education*, Dr. Glen Schultz, a Christian educator, says, "At the foundation of a person's life we find his beliefs. These beliefs shape his values, and his values drive his actions."[4] Obviously, parents are concerned with what their kids could be tempted to do, but of greater concern should be what their children believe because that will determine their behavior, attitudes, and eventually choices they make in life. "Even children are known by the way they act, whether their conduct is pure and right" (Prov. 20:11, NLT). Teaching a moral and ethical code of conduct is a process that begins at birth and continues throughout the life of your children.

Values involve more than just a set of rules; they also involve a change of heart. Unless the heart is changed, both ours and our children's, regulations will be cast off at some time in their life. Josh McDowell states in his book *Beyond Belief to Convictions* that the belief system of our youth is in crisis. He feels that while many of our kids may be taking a "pragmatic stand" for some good things, however, the way they determine what is true and good is alarming. "Today's culture encourages our young people to 'figure it out' themselves, and what most are 'figuring out' is a little truth here and a little error there until they end up with erroneous beliefs. Most of them are not looking to a biblical test for truth; they are actually looking within themselves. The majority of youth (70 percent) say there is no absolute moral truth."[5] He goes on to state, based on a study by Barna Research Group, that 72 percent of our teens believe that "you can tell if something is morally/ethically right for you by whether or not it works in your life."[6] Fraud today is rampant, such as stealing from the company, lying to your employer, or falsifying the company's records. These fraudulent activities "work in your life for a while," but sooner or later truth will percolate to the surface and be exposed. "He who conceals his sins does not prosper, but whoever confesses and renounces them finds mercy" (Prov. 28:13, NIV).

Webster defines *integrity* as "virtue tested and approved; uprightness of character; honesty; complete and undivided." Tom, my dear friend and spiritual dad, a father of six children in a blended family, and former business owner, shared the following thoughts about integrity in the home. "Integrity is not something we acquire, but it is a way of life. The way is complete and undivided. We cannot be double minded; that is, doing the right thing one moment and the wrong thing the next, depending upon the circumstances. There is no compromise in integrity, not even little white lies. We cannot teach our children integrity by merely expressing it in words, but by living it out day by day under the watchful gaze of innocent eyes."

One meaning of integrity is "virtue tested and confirmed," and the confirmation will come from our children and others who observe our life and find out we really *do* what we say. Integrity is strict, no compromise. We teach our children by example, and they need to see honor and integrity exemplified in a practical way in the home. We should find ways to be transparent and let our families know when it is a struggle to make the right choices to be honest and truthful. As parents, we must first have the spiritual insight before we will be able to guide our children into this type of wisdom. We are encouraged in Psalm 139 to ask this of the Lord: "Search me, O God, and know my heart; test me and know my thoughts. Point out anything in me that offends you, and lead me along the path of everlasting life" (Ps. 139:23–24, NLT). The Scriptures also give instruction to young people about following the wisdom and guidance of their parents. "Listen, my child, to what your father teaches you. Don't neglect your mother's teaching. What you learn from them will crown you with grace and clothe you with honor" (Prov. 1:8–9, NLT). Again in the New Testament, Ephesians 6:1 says, "Children, obey your parents because you belong to the Lord, for this is the right thing to do" (NLT). The Scriptures give clear guidelines and instruction, to both parents and children, for success in outlining and following the path of integrity. The question is, will we have enough faith to trust in God and His promises to translate those beliefs into a plan of action to be implemented in the home.

Integrity training in the home can be compared to the internal control environment in a corporate setting as described in chapter five regarding the COSO model. The corporate world describes integrity and ethical values as follows: "Management must convey the message that integrity and ethical values cannot be compromised, and employees must receive and understand that message. Management must continually demonstrate, through words and actions, a commitment to high ethical standards" as mandated in the COSO model. There are several levels of control that must be observed in the business environment, and so it is in training our children. Each age will require a slightly different approach, but the common thread for every stage of development is *prayer*. We must pray for our children and ask the Lord to show us how we can best guide them into moral and ethical living.

I began praying the following twelve points of prayer for my son at the beginning of his eighth grade year and continue to do so even now. Perhaps they will be helpful for you as well.

1. Come to know Christ as your personal Savior early in life (Ps. 63:1).

2. Have a hatred for sin (Ps. 97:10).

3. Be caught when guilty (Ps. 119:71).

4. Be emotionally, physically, and spiritually protected from the devil (John 17:15).

5. Have a responsible attitude (Dan. 6:3–4).

6. Respect those in authority (Rom. 13:1).

7. Desire the right kind of friends and be protected from wrong ones (Prov. 1:10, 15).

8. Be kept from the wrong mate and kept for the right one (2 Cor. 6:14).

9. Be kept pure until marriage (1 Cor. 6:18–20).

10. Learn to submit to God, and actively resist Satan (James 4:7).

11. Be single-hearted, willing to be sold out to Jesus (Rom. 12:11–12).

12. Be hedged in (surrounded) to where you cannot find your way to wrong people and places, and wrong people cannot find you (Hosea 2:6).

This may seem like a weighty prayer list, but I have been able to see these things worked out in my son's life through the years. You have God's promise to give you wisdom if you will ask for it.

For the LORD grants wisdom! From his mouth come knowledge and understanding. He grants

a treasure of good sense to the godly. He is their
shield, protecting those who walk with integrity.
He guards the paths of justice and protects those
who are faithful to him. Then you will understand
what is right, just, and fair, and you will know how
to find the right course of action every time. For
wisdom will enter your heart, and knowledge will
fill you with joy. Wise planning will watch over
you. Understanding will keep you safe.
—PROVERBS 2:6–11, NLT

Truth remains constant, but how a parent discloses and encourages a child to embrace the truth can take many avenues. Early
childhood is perhaps the easiest years to instill truth and values in
children, and yet these years are the most crucial because they lay
the groundwork for success in the more difficult years that will follow. A young child's mind is like a sponge, absorbing everything it
comes in contact with. Harmless or lethal, it makes no difference;
the substance will be absorbed. We noted earlier that the heart is like
soil for planting. Obviously, the reference is not to the physical heart
but refers to the Hebrew meaning, "center of the being." Craig Hill,
founder of Family Foundations International, gives the following
definitions of the heart based upon the truth of Scripture.

- The heart is the production center of the
  thoughts, emotions, and choices. It is the seat
  of the soul (Heb. 4:12).

- The heart is a "filter" between the impulses of
  the spirit and the flesh.

- The heart is a storehouse of treasures, good or
  evil (Luke 6:45; Mark 7:20–23).

If these principles are true, then we can see the gravity of planting seeds of right living first into our own hearts and then into the

hearts of our children. That planting, when properly cultivated, will bring a harvest of integrity. It is this integrity that will manifest itself years later in the work environment. This is not the stage of training in which we allow our children to choose for themselves the information they assimilate. We must chose for them the values that will set the precedence for their future. "Train is a word of deep importance for every parent to understand. Training is not telling, not teaching, not commanding, but something higher than all these (without which the teaching and commanding often does more harm than good). It is not only telling a child what to do but also showing him how to do it and then seeing that is done, taking care that the advice or the command given is put into practice and adopted as a habit."[7]

At a Bill Glass prison outreach, Weekend of Champions, Bill Glass shared the following story that clearly represents integrity training. Bill and his sons were out hunting one night on their Texas ranch when a beautiful fourteen-point buck came clearly into their line of vision. As the deer stood motionless in the truck's glaring spotlight, the first impulse was to bag the magnificent trophy. There were two slight problems: It was not deer season, and a hunter cannot shoot a deer at night. To do so would have been a violation of the law even though no one would have known. The deer survived. Bill used this opportunity to teach respect for authority and to exemplify personal integrity to his children.

These kinds of clear lessons will stay with them for the rest of their lives.

How can we neglect this weighty responsibility to train up our children in a structured environment that will produce obedience, honor, and respect for others?

There are many ways to implement good training in the home— the bedrock that will shape your child's behavior in the ensuing years. The following checklist may inspire some creative ideas:

- Daily reading of Scripture or some related Bible story

- Memorization of Scripture verses that are relevant to the needs of the child

- Prayer at the dinner table—teach your child to be thankful.

- Church attendance and fellowship with children/youth in their age group

- Summer camps where good values and moral character are stressed

- Invite guests into your home that will influence your children positively. Missionaries are especially interesting.

- Introduce uplifting/spiritual music to the home. Songs (both good and bad) will remain in the memory for a lifetime. This is also a great way to memorize Scripture verses.

- Encourage genuine worship. Cultivate an awareness of God in your child.

- Read biographies of famous and successful people of good character to your young children. Make materials such as this available for your older children to read.

- Require your children to work in the home. Teach them that money is not the greatest reward for a job well done.

- Children should be taught to give to others and to tithe in obedience to Scripture. This includes their possessions and their time.

- Some families educate their children in a

Christian school; however, this is to support the teaching already provided in the home.

- Expect obedience; it is not optional.

- Use negative situations as an opportunity to teach, not to condemn.

- Most importantly, be consistent.

This list highlights only a few of ways we can direct the course of our children's lives. Every home should have their own unique plan based on scriptural values and insights and consistently put this plan into practice. "My child, how I rejoice if you become wise. Yes, my heart will thrill when you speak what is right and just" (Prov. 23:15–16, NLT).

We tried to implement many things from the list above as we reared our son, Matt. Although far from perfect, he embraces much of what he learned in his formidable years. Perhaps the most noteworthy example of the influence of early training is my discovery of how Matt was inspired from the Book of Proverbs. Beginning in the ninth grade, we made an effort to read a chapter from Proverbs every morning at breakfast. I read, and Matt listened while he ate. This continued through the better part of high school. One day while cleaning his room, I happened to pick up the Bible on his nightstand and flip through the pages. What a blessing to find the Book of Proverbs was underlined and highlighted on almost every page. It is my firm belief that he is of such noble character today because of the influence of Scripture in his life. Never underestimate the power of truth in the life of your child, especially if that truth is based on the written Word of God.

My son, obey your father's commands, and don't neglect your mother's teaching. Keep their words always in your heart. Tie them around your neck. Wherever you walk their counsel can lead you.

When you sleep, they will protect you. When you wake up in the morning, they will advise you. For these commands and this teaching are a lamp to light the way ahead of you. The correction of discipline is the way to life.

—PROVERBS 6:20–23, NLT

The best measure of a man's honesty isn't his income tax return. It's the zero adjust on his bathroom scale.

—Arthur C. Clarke

CHAPTER 8

Responsibilities in the Workplace
by Mary A. Steelman

Business was the worst it had been in several years. The loss of the company's largest account in addition to the new tax laws had dramatically reduced the company's bottom line. Still, Mr. Smith did not have the right to cut everyone's salary and reduce many of their benefits. The company assured everyone that when times were better, everything—and more—would be restored.

"Right," Bob muttered under his breath as he reviewed all that had transpired over the last year. He wanted to believe things would be better, but his gut feeling told him something different. After all, he was the company's chief accountant and painstakingly maintained the accounting records. Recovery did not appear to be around the corner. He had tried to tell Mr. Smith not to make those investments, but his conservative counsel was ignored.

Instead, his boss had chosen to follow the advice of Stu, Smith Manufacturing's new investment advisor. Stu just happened to be Mr. Smith's favorite nephew who recently graduated from one of the top business schools and "needed some experience under his belt" to prepare him for the real world. With little practical experience, Stu had persuaded his uncle to make some investments that would, in Bob's opinion, jeopardize the company's financial integrity. Mr. Smith had always displayed such wisdom and honor in his decisions, and this "scheme" was so unlike him. Stu's arrogance and pride made Bob a bit hot under the collar, and he tried to make allowances for his youth and inexperience, but each day brought another opportunity for disagreement and offense.

"If Stu had my financial responsibilities, he wouldn't be so free with his uncle's hard-earned money," Bob mumbled to himself as he thought of the difficult circumstances he was facing.

Sandy's prolonged illness had created a real hardship on the family, and Bob was facing the full weight of the financial responsibility. She had worked as a RN since they were first married, and the loss of a second income had really taken its toll on the family's finances. The kids also had needs, and Bob did not want them to feel the pressure and embarrassment of a lack of money to maintain their lifestyles. Now everything was coming due with few funds available. Bob tried to suppress the rising thoughts of panic; however, deep inside he knew he was in serious financial trouble.

How embarrassing to be a seasoned accountant and find yourself in such a dilemma. Bob had sought counsel from his parents, and they offered the same old solutions. "Turn back to the training you learned as a child, Bob. You know the foundational truths of Scripture will keep you on the right path," his dad had reminded him. After listening to several encouraging scriptures, Bob left his parents' home with a renewed sense of well-being and focus on ethics. However, today's pressure seemed to be too overwhelming to conquer as Bob struggled with a thought even he was ashamed to admit.

As Bob opened the accounts receivable files on the Johnson account, he wished he had not discovered the error that was glaring at him at from the spreadsheet. How easy it would be to adjust a few numbers and slip the extra income into his pocket. After all, Smith Manufacturing may never know, and his personal financial needs would be relieved, at least for the time being, by "lapping receivables." He had been a faithful employee for many years, and Bob was trying to convince himself that he deserved a little extra compensation, especially under his current circumstances.

As Bob sat struggling with the idea, a sense of uneasiness began to sweep over him. He recognized the gentle but familiar voice that was speaking to his conscience about his impending decision to commit fraud. Bob recalled sitting in church as a teen the day his pastor had preached on overcoming temptation and how a person had to rely upon the strength of the Lord for help. As the pastor openly shared some of his own struggles with temptation as well as his victory over them, Bob listened intently, appreciating the fact that his pastor was willing to be transparent. He was especially captivated by the verse from 1 Corinthians that had helped the pastor overcome his temptations. Bob had even memorized the verse and shared it with others who needed it. It had been a long time since he had thought about that verse, but the Holy Spirit was prompting his memory word by word.

> But remember that the temptations that come into your life are no different from what others experience. And God is faithful. He will keep the temptation from becoming so strong that you can't stand up to it. When you are tempted, he will show you a way out so that you will not give in to it.
> —1 Corinthians 10:13, nlt

Bob's heart softened as he began to recall the many verses he had learned early in his life. He had observed his mother and father, as well as many other influential people in his life, following the principles of integrity found in many of those scriptures even in difficult times. At that moment, Bob knew he would make the right choice, a choice that would bring integrity to himself and Smith Manufacturing.

Although the story you just read is fictional, the fact is that, in the past, more accounting professionals felt pressured to do the wrong thing versus doing what is right. With the implementation of the law, we are seeing a move toward integrity, but a change of the heart is what we need.

It's the Law

In an interview on CBS's *60 Minutes,* Dr. Sam Waksal, CEO for ImClone Systems Inc., was asked the following question: "What have you learned from this experience?" His answer: "Never break the law." Dr. Waksal plead guilty to illegal insider trading. He stated that he had acted irresponsibly and had a long record of indiscretions. Cutting corners had been a way of life for Sam Waksal according to the interviewer. However, when asked how he now views himself, Dr. Waksal stated he "thinks of himself as doing good things for society."[1]

Doing good things for society is wonderful, but good deeds never take the place of truth, honesty, and integrity, even with the best intentions. Dr. Bob Jones Sr., founder of Bob Jones University, often reminded the students that "it is never right to do wrong in order to get a chance to do right."

Sam Waksal will spend several years in prison for decisions he regrets.

The temptation to cheat is prevalent in all walks of life and cannot be embraced as an option. The prophet Isaiah gave clear instruction to Israel when he wrote:

> ...those who are honest and fair, who reject making a profit by fraud, who stay far away from bribes, who refuse to listen to whose who plot murder, who shut their eyes to all enticement to do wrong. These are the ones who will dwell on high. The rocks of the mountains will be their fortress of safety. Food will be supplied to them, and they will have water in abundance.
>
> —Isaiah 33:15–16, NLT

Scripture is as relevant today as when it was first penned and we can rely upon the validity of its instruction. Dr. Mark Rutland, president of Southeastern College in Lakeland, Florida, shared the following thoughts about dishonesty:

> The motivation for dishonesty is the animal instinct for self-preservation. The flesh says, "If I want it, I'll

steal it. If I am not, I'll pretend to be. If I am, I'll pretend not to be. If I want to sell it, I will not tell everything." What can possibly shatter the spell of so "inborn an instinct?"[2]

Was it that inborn instinct that led Sam Waksal to betray his company and include himself among the many white-collar offenders? Sam Waksal, like many others, failed to see the truth found in Proverbs 22:4: "By humility and fear of the LORD are riches, and honour, and life" (KJV).

Both the employer and employee have a biblical mandate with regard to the working relationship.

Employer Responsibilities

It is your responsibility as an employer to oversee the safety of your employees. It is also your responsibility to maintain a good working relationship with them. Your current position as the authority figure in the company is not happenstance; it was a divine mandate. It is up to you whether or not you will follow the guidelines outlined for you in the Scriptures.

> And you, masters, do the same things to them, giving up threatening, knowing that your own Master also is in heaven, and there is no partiality in Him.
>
> —EPHESIANS 6:9

Master in this context comes from the original Greek word *kurios*, which means "the owner; one who has control of the person."[3] As an employer, the government requires you to be impartial and provide a nonthreatening environment. The human resource laws involving harassment and discrimination are nothing new. They have their roots in God's Word, as clearly outlined in Ephesians 6:9.

Employers have certain responsibilities to their employees. Although the responsibilities are many, great care should be taken to create an atmosphere of integrity, trust, and loyalty within a company, that is, setting "Tone at the Top." Fair wages, good benefits, opportunities for advancement, safe working environment, and so on are all essential in establishing good employee/employer relationships.

As an employer, seize the opportunity to be a blessing and an encouragement to everyone in your employment.

Employee Responsibilities

If you're an employee, you too have responsibilities to your employer.

> Bondservants, be obedient to those who are your masters according to the flesh, with fear and trembling, in sincerity of heart, as to Christ; not with eyeservice, as men-pleasers, but as bondservants of Christ, doing the will of God from the heart, with goodwill doing service, as to the Lord, and not to men, knowing that whatever good anyone does, he will receive the same from the Lord.
>
> —EPHESIANS 6:5–8

Honesty tops the list of expectations for employees—honesty in both words and deeds. Other virtues such as loyalty, dependability, humility, a teachable spirit, and respect are also high on the list of an employer as he searches for potential employees to help him in building a successful and prosperous business.

Too often people are eager to do the "right" thing when the supervisor is watching, yet they neglect to continue doing the "right" thing even when he or she is not watching closely. For example, the correct thing to do is:

- Get to work on time.

- Do not take office supplies (not even a pen).

- Do not use work time to accomplish personal tasks.

- Use the phone for business only and not personal calls.

If you keep in mind that you are working for a Higher Authority, knowing that you will have to answer to Him, you are more likely to raise your standard of accountability.

Likewise, employees are looking for ethical leadership that will provide security, honesty, and integrity in the workplace.

Honesty *Is* the Best Policy

Baylor University President Rufus C. Burleson once told an audience:

> How often I have heard my father paint in glowing words the honesty of his old friend Colonel Ben Sherrod. When he was threatened with bankruptcy and destitution in old age and was staggering under a debt of $850,000, a contemptible lawyer told him, "Colonel Sherrod, you are hopelessly ruined, but if you will furnish me five thousand dollars as a witness fee, I can pick a technical flaw in the whole thing and get you out of it." The grand old Alabamian replied, "Your proposition is insulting. I signed the notes in good faith, and the last dollar shall be paid if charity digs my grave and buys my shroud." It's the natural thing to want to find the easiest, least implicating means out of a tough situation. Yet what is at first difficult will be an asset later when people think about your integrity and character. The people you work with will remember you for the promises you keep and truth you tell— especially at times when you could have profited from distorting or hiding the truth. Your character is your greatest asset, and your honesty is your most valuable currency.[4]

As stated in chapter seven, integrity is a matter of the heart and should be based on solid scriptural values that do not change. Methods may change, but the Truth does not. In a massive opinion survey called "The Day America Told the Truth," James Patterson and Peter Kim reported some shocking findings:[5]

- Only 13 percent of Americans saw all Ten Commandments as biding and relevant.

- Ninety-one percent lied regularly, both at work and home.

- Most workers admitted to "goofing off" for an average of seven hours each week.

- About half of the work force admitted they regularly called in sick when they were in fact healthy.

- Further, when asked what they would be willing to do for $10 million, 25 percent said they would abandon their families, 23 percent would be prostitutes for a week, and 7 percent would murder a stranger.

What a sad representation of the lack of values in today's society especially as it relates to the workplace. If people do not have integrity in their places of business, they probably will not have it anywhere else. The Sarbanes-Oxley Act is an effort on the part of our government to restore ethics to American corporations. If administered correctly, this country could embark upon a tremendous reformation. In any organization, reform starts at the top and filters down through the entire company. Employers must personally engage in active measures of reform if they are to see renewal take place in their employees.

Proverbs 11:1 says, "The LORD hates cheating, but he delights in honesty" (NLT). In ancient cultures, scales were used in many business transactions. If a merchant was dishonest, he would often fix his measures to gain more profit. Wealth was of greater value to him than the welfare of others or his own reputation. Scripture tells us that a good name is to be chosen over great riches (Prov. 22:1), and the Lord insists that His people be honest in their dealings.

I am reminded of a story of two co-workers debating over which translation of the Bible was the most accurate. After reaching an impasse, they decided to ask the opinion of another worker. His response, "Well, I really like my boss's translation. You see, my boss has translated the pages of the Bible into his life. He has lived the message, and it has been the most convincing translation I have ever witnessed." The apostle Paul had the same idea when he wrote these words of encouragement to the Philippian church: "Keep putting into practice all you learned from me and heard from me and saw me doing, and the God of peace will be with you" (Phil. 4:9, NLT). Honesty must be the cornerstone of the employer/employee work relationship if there is to be a renewal of integrity in the corporations of America.

James II. Amos Jr., former CEO for Mail Boxes, Etc., said it best as he shared his beliefs on the true purpose of a company.

> What [I] do believe is that the number one purpose of business is to build character in others, to assist in raising people to a higher level of performance, excellence, and morals. Isn't that what Christ did with His disciples and with those He touched? Making money ought to be a by-product of building the character of men and women and rendering essential service to others. Profits come and go, but character is eternal. Developing Christlikeness in each other is more important than making money. If we do these things, it is my firm belief that the

profit will take care of itself, not just in the short term or quantities, but in the long term as well. Everyone has influence over other people every day. Changing lives and growing people should take precedence over making money.[6]

As an employer, seize the opportunity to be a blessing and encouragement to everyone in your employment.

ETHICS
ETHICS

Truth stands the test of time; lies are soon exposed.

—PROVERBS 12:19, NLT

ETHICS

CHAPTER 9

Beyond Sarbanes-Oxley

A bridge to reformation in the future in which we view our business practices from a biblical ethics perspective will be a true "Best Practice." We must look beyond the Sarbanes-Oxley Act and challenge the consciences of men and women to formulate decision making based on righteous thinking. This will not be an easy task. It will take great focus and concentration, but with God's help it can be done. The future of our nation's business industry hangs in the balance.

I recently viewed a documentary on the epic story of Sir Ernest Shackleton's 1914 "Endurance Expedition to the Antarctic." This daunting expedition to a continent challenged every fiber of these men as they weathered the freezing elements for nearly two years. (Having spent a few days in Patagonia in southern Chile, I had a small taste of what their endurance must have been like.)

Our ability to correct the course we are on in Corporate America is not unlike what Shackleton and his men went through in 1914. This process of reformation is deep and difficult and will take time. Our economic future is dependent on successfully effecting such a reformation.

"Turning the Sunday stuff into Monday stuff for better lives and better business" is the theme promulgated by a fascinating group of business leaders called BBL (Beyond the Bottom Line), based in Southern California. (See the Web site www.bblforum.com.) Their focus on transforming biblical principles into business solutions is right on point as we drive toward Reformation in Corporate America.

BBL and groups like it will be the lynchpin to driving change deep into the business ethics of our nation.

Randy Cohen, writer for the *New York Times* magazine, states:

> Governance, like religion, does not attract followers in good times. And as stocks soared in the late '90s, CEOs became more imperial than ever. But after an unprecedented run of scandal, people noticed that boards had been in a position to thwart the mischief; yet instead, they enabled it. At Enron, the board waived its rule against conflicts of interest for executives and knowingly allowed the executives to doctor the earnings. At WorldCom, the board permitted Bernie Ebbers to "borrow" $400 million. The obvious conclusion was that if Bernie Ebbers could not be reformed, his board had to be. One of the few people who did not seem alarmed was Richard Grasso. He repeatedly exclaimed, "For every Enron, there are 1,000 Exxons."[1]

In fact, hundreds of other companies have had to admit to reporting bogus earnings. Few of them could have gotten away with it had their boards' audit committees taken their role seriously.

Sarbanes-Oxley is certainly a healthy step forward, albeit driven by federal regulators who do not necessarily subscribe to any particular religious basis. But more is needed as follows:

- As discussed in chapter seven, "Integrity Begins at Home," we must establish, with the help of the church, a continuum of biblical business ethics training for the home, the school, and the church on an ongoing basis within Corporate America.

- We should clearly set forth in our corporate mission statements the religious beliefs for

which our codes of conduct are shaped—
hopefully on a biblical basis.

- We should embed within our corporate ethics
  training support for those codes of conduct.

- We should financially and otherwise reward
  those who follow such codes of conduct in a
  manner to encourage others to do so also.

In a *BusinessWeek* editorial, "Corporate Governance: The Road
Back," it was noted:

> A new era of reform is dawning for Corporate
> America. Sparked by a popular revolt of the inves-
> tor class driven by a Republican Administration
> surprisingly intent on change, this movement aims
> to restore core American values of fairness, equity
> and responsibility to the practice of big business
> in the U.S. Because the reform impulse is coming
> from the center and the right, generally sympathetic
> to business, the demand for change is all the more
> potent. It cannot be ignored.
>
> The magnitude of this movement has been
> underestimated by many chief executives. They
> fail to see that the accumulation of indictments,
> investigations, financial restatements, conflicts of
> interest, and examples of executive greed had led
> to a major breach of trust between the public and
> business leaders. Those CEOs who dismiss the push
> for reform as merely a temporary down-market phe-
> nomenon or overreaction to Enron Corp. risk hurt-
> ing themselves, their corporations and the nation. If
> confidence in Corporate America's leadership is not
> quickly restored, the equity culture that generated so
> much wealth in the '90s will dissipate.

The last time the impulse to reform Big Business came from the center-right was at the turn of 20th Century under Theodore Roosevelt. Then, Roosevelt railed against the institution of the giant monopoly trust and the risk it posed to American democratic values. Today, President George W. Bush is on TV criticizing not the corporation per se, but the values held by the business elite. It is the failure of far too many CEOs, board members, accountants, analysts and lawyers to take personal responsibility, to act with integrity, to be fair and equitable, that makes the reform effort so much a conservative movement about values.[2]

Within my own profession, we must live up to and revise as necessary the codes of ethics we are sworn to follow as CPAs. No other profession can do more to insist on "doing the right thing" than the public accounting industry. CPAs answer to a higher calling than partnership profits!

In *CFO Magazine* Andrew Osterland reported:

> For corporate executives, that defensive mode already means tougher, more expensive audits and less wiggle room when it comes to the interpretation of accounting rules....The Sarbanes-Oxley Act is no immediate cure for a deeply shaken market, but it may go a long way toward fostering a more independent and adversarial role for audits of public companies.[3]

The effect will not be inexpensive. PwC senior partner Sam DiPiazza, who recently testified before a government panel as described in the *Financial Times*, said:

> For our US firms, practice protection costs are now the second largest cost of doing business, second only to the compensation provided to its people.[4]

An article on *BusinessWeek* online, entitled "Honesty Is a Pricey Policy," reiterated the cost of doing business with integrity and honesty.

> Industry experts say that as a result of these rules, auditing costs are likely to double, while the total tab for compliance could top $7 billion in the first year. Although most big companies can afford to pay, the costs could push some smaller companies into the red....What's worse, the bulk of the extra expenses won't be one-shot outlays—say, for auditing templates—but will be incurred annually. For instance, the rules call for auditors to test systems every year, even if they haven't been changed.[5]

The financial cost will undoubtedly distract Corporate America from focusing on the root problem—lack of integrity—and moving toward the solution. Only when men and women have a change of heart and make the choice to conduct business using biblically based decisions will they be able to conduct business in an ethical manner. It is then that Reformation in Corporate America will take place.

The challenge with SOX is that we will default into only looking at this as a "mechanical" exercise and fail to remember that it all started with the misdeeds of men and women at Enron, WorldCom, Adelphia, Arthur Andersen, and so on.

As an example, a recent ACIPA National SEC Conference in December 2003, in Washington, DC, highlighted SOX comments from an SEC registrant as follows:

Public Companies Perception of Sarbanes-Oxley (SOX)

O Most of Sarbanes-Oxley is "Best in Class" corporate governance, which we are already doing.

○ We applaud the focus on auditor independence, corporate responsibility, code of ethics,
audit committee financial expert, and penalties for intentional wrongdoing.

○ It provides leverage and support to focus on
business controls. You put Sarbanes in front
of a request, and the barriers seem to disap-
pear.

○ SOX 404 has some very positive focus on
internal controls, but the overwhelming belief
is that it is overkill and that the shareholders
at some point will not get the incremental
payback from the tremendous investment
being spent on internal controls.

What Does SOX 404 Mean to Public Companies?

○ Companies do have stronger and better
documented internal controls.

○ Other functions outside of finance have a
better understanding of what effective internal controls really entail.

○ Order administrators to senior vice presi-
dents are engaged in the overall business
environment at a lower level of detail than in
the past.

○ Audit committees are more active in understanding the current state of the company's
internal controls.

Negative Impact

- ◐ A survey prior to the release of the proposed standard showed multinational spending 25,000–50,000 hours of internal/external time implementing SOX 404. With the release of exposure draft, that has to go up.

- ◐ Spending is in the millions of dollars to cover consultants and the 25–50 percent proposed increases in external audit fees alone.

- ◐ The potentially significant increase in testing and monitoring from process owners and internal audit and CPA firms is expected to be very disruptive and hurt the productivity of the processes.

At this SOX conference, there was very little deep discussion of business ethics (even though COSO requires it). Rather, there were extensive details and debate about the implementation of these new federal regulations. Accordingly, we are doomed to repeat the sins of the past if we continue to be blind to the deceit of executives, whose moral temperature is below the freezing mark.

Section 404 of SOX is starting to show its muscle. In early 2004, the *Wall Street Journal* reported that the Swiss-based temporary staffing company, Adecco SA, uncovered significant issues with revenue recognition, computer systems security, payroll bank accounts, irregularities regarding cash applications to accounting receivable at the North American headquarters, which brought about the termination of certain executives.

On January 12, Adecco disclosed that a number of problems, including "material weaknesses" in the internal controls in North America, meant it

wouldn't publish its 2003 financial results as sched-
uled on February 4.[6]

This is just one of many examples of the impact Section 404 is
having on Corporate America, and we should expect more of this
over the next few years.

The PCAOB will demand a lot more of this profession over the
next few years. There will be a lot of pain before the vaccine takes
effect.

But the reformation will be successful if we build it on a foundation of biblical ethics and continuous respect and training of those
ethics to our children and employees.

If the LORD *delights in a man's way, he makes his steps firm.*

—PSALM 37:23, NIV

C H A P T E R   1 0

It's All About Character and Integrity

It is encouraging to see changes starting in this post-Enron era within the corporate world regarding the emphasis on character and integrity. Many companies have the best of intentions to instill integrity and higher ethical standards into their top-level executives. Most of these companies are genuine in their efforts to win back the trust of consumers, and that is a good place to start. The "good deeds," however encouraging they are, cannot replace a changed attitude and heart. All of these efforts merely address the outer layer of the problem. It's like trying to put a Band-Aid on a deep wound. In order for true change to take place, surgery needs to take place—it's a matter of character and integrity.

Even as we see this progress, we must keep in mind that there is a constant battle to "do the right thing." For example, the *Wall Street Journal* disclosed that in December 2003 and January 2004, PricewaterhouseCoopers was struggling internally with the issue of the application of travel rebates for large block purchases of air travel and how to distribute the savings to their clients. The internal struggle within its own internal ethics department is an excellent example of why this book is written. The need for biblically based decision making is critical to the long-term success and reputation of all enterprises. PwC paid a price in terms of settlements and suffered some effect on its reputation from this issue.[1]

Joseph Berardino, senior partner of Arthur Andersen, disclosed to *BusinessWeek*, "I paid the price, I lost my job. I lost my firm.... I lost my retirement.... I may never work again."[2] Those powerful words show the despair and troubled heart that exists within Corporate America. The troubles encountered in companies such as Tyco, Freddie Mac, Enron, and Adelphia, to name a few, strongly suggest that we need a Reformation in Corporate America like never before.

Time for the 3 R's

Now is the time for our nation to "get back to the basics" in corporate society through *repentance*, *renewal*, and *reformation*.

This is a time of repentance.

Our pride in a multi-trillion dollar economy has led us to believe we are somehow above reproach. As the writer of Proverbs 16:18 says, "Pride goes before destruction, and a haughty spirit before a fall." Pride and greed have led to the meltdown of many businesses, but humility and integrity are the "high road" to recovery. This is not the time for us to become judgmental toward any corporate entity or individual, but rather take responsibility and ownership for our mistakes.

We should look at this opportunity as a time to repent of our wrongdoings and know that God hears us. All we need to do is simply ask.

Ask Jesus Christ to forgive you of your sins and enter your heart. Perhaps you feel "unworthy" or think that you can't invite Jesus Christ into your life because of the things you've done. (See Matthew 7:7–12.) The truth is, *everyone* is unworthy. Jesus clearly said, "I have not come to call the righteous, but sinners, to repentance" (Luke 5:32). There is nothing you can do in your own strength to "get right," nor does "being a good person" save you.

> God saved you by his special favor when you be-
> lieved. And you can't take credit for this; it is a gift
> from God. Salvation is not a reward for the good
> things we have done, so none of us can boast about
> it.
>
> —Ephesians 2:8–9, NLT

You may ask yourself, *So what must I do?* The formula is a simple one: (a) confess Jesus Christ as Lord of your life, (b) believe with your heart that God raised Jesus Christ from the dead, and (c) you are saved.

> For with the heart one believes unto righteousness, and with the mouth confession is made unto salvation.
>
> —ROMANS 10:10

Pray this simple prayer:

> *Dear God,*
>
> *I acknowledge that I have not lived a life that is pleasing to You. I repent of my sins, and I confess that Jesus Christ is Lord of my life. I do believe that on that resurrection day You raised Jesus from the dead.*
>
> *Jesus, I invite You to come into my heart and be a part of my life. I give You the lordship over my life. Thank You for dying on the cross for my sins and redeeming my life. You paid the price for me. In Jesus' name, amen.*

If we can help you in this regard, please feel free to contact us at our Web site, www.integrityadvisorsinc.com.

This is a time for renewal.

Our country is embattled with issues from terrorism to life-threatening illnesses, but we are a resilient nation. Part of that resiliency can be attributed to the fact that the Founding Fathers built the laws of this land upon biblical principles. We need to renew the foundational principles that were once exercised in our board meeting rooms. We also need to renew the faith that so many people have lost in our accounting system.

This is a time for reformation.

Some good has emerged from the financial rubble of Wall Street, although it may not appear so on the surface. The downfall of so many companies was a clarion call to everyone—from the CEO to the small-time investor—to change dramatically the way we've done business in the past. It's a call to a higher level of ethical values that must begin within the heart of every individual. It is time to reform the way we conduct business. The time is now for a biblical reformation!

Building a Bridge to the Future

The bridge to the future is built on the Word of God and our dedication to it. This process is a lifetime of commitment to godly decision making. The study of ethics principles should not be without a biblical emphasis and a dedication to doing "right" in the eyes of God and looking for His blessings for that obedience.

Over the years, I have often thought of another reformer, Martin Luther. As a high school senior, my class memorized and quoted at our graduation all the stanzas of Luther's hymn "A Mighty Fortress Is Our God."

> A mighty fortress is our God, a bulwark never failing;
> Our helper He amid the flood of mortal ills prevaling.
> For still our ancient foe doth seek to work us woe;
> His craft and power are great, and armed with cruel hate,
> On earth is not his equal.
>
> Did we in our own strength confide, our striving would be losing;
> Were not the right Man on our side, the Man of God's own choosing.
> Dost ask who that may be? Christ Jesus, it is He;
> Lord Sabbaoth, His Name, from age to age the same,
> And He must win the battle.

And though this world, with devils filled, should
    threaten to undo us,
We will not fear, for God hath willed His truth to
    triumph through us.
The Prince of Darkness grim, we tremble not for
    him;
His rage we can endure, for lo, his doom is sure
One little word shall fell him.

That word above all earthly powers, no thanks to
    them, abideth;
The Spirit and the gifts are ours, thru Him Who
    with us sideth.
Let goods and kindred go, this mortal life also;
The body they may kill; God's truth abideth still;
His kingdom is forever.

The biblical wisdom in these words has kept me focused on the strength of God's Word as I travel through life. It's all about character and integrity.

APPENDIX I

Sarbanes-Oxley Act of 2002
Sectional Outline

	Original Effective Date
1. Public Company Accounting Oversight Board	
101 Establishment; administrative provisions (PCAOB)	4/26/03
102 Registration with the Board	10/26/03
103 Auditing, quality control, and independence standards and rules (e.g., New Standards)	Pending
104 Inspections of registered public accounting firms	Every 3 years
105 Investigations and disciplinary proceedings	7/30/02
106 Foreign public accounting firms (e.g., foreign firms subject to SOA)	7/30/02
107 Commission oversight of the Board (e.g., SEC oversees PCAOB)	7/30/02
108 Accounting standards (e.g., PCAOB will rely on FASB)	7/30/02
109 Funding	7/30/02
2. Auditor Independence	
201 Services outside the scope of practice of auditors	5/6/03
202 Pre-approval requirements (e.g., audit committee pre-approves audit/non-audit svcs.)	5/6/03
203 Audit partner rotation	5/6/03
204 Auditor reports to audit committee	5/6/03
205 Conforming amendments	7/30/02
206 Conflicts of interest	5/6/03
207 Study of mandatory rotation of registered public accounting firms	7/30/02
208 Commission authority	7/30/02
209 Considerations by appropriate state regulatory authorities	7/30/02

	Original Effective Date
3. Corporate Responsibility	
301 Public company audit committees	4/26/04
302 Corporate responsibility for financial reports	8/29/02
303 Improper influence on conduct of audits	7/30/02
304 Forfeiture of certain bonuses and profits	7/30/02
305 Officer and director bars and penalties	7/30/02
306 Insider trades during pension fund blackout periods	1/26/03
307 Rules of professional responsibility for attorneys	8/5/03
308 Fair funds for investors	7/30/02
4. Enhanced Financial Disclosures	
401 Disclosures in periodic reports	
401a Off-balance sheet arrangements and contractual obligations	6/15/03
401b Non-GAAP financial measures	3/28/03
401c Study and report on special purpose entities	NA
402 Enhanced conflict of interest provisions	7/30/02
403 Disclosures of transactions involving management and principal stockholders	8/29/02
404 Management assessment of internal controls—75M Market Cap	6/15/04
404 Management assessment of internal controls—Below 75M Market Cap	4/15/05
405 Exemption	7/30/02
406 Code of ethics for senior financial officers	7/15/03
407 Disclosure of audit committee financial expert	7/15/03
407 Disclosure of audit committee financial expert—small business issuers	12/15/03
408 Enhanced review of periodic disclosures by issuers	7/30/02
409 Real-time issuer disclosures	7/30/02
5. Analyst Conflicts of Interest	
501 Treatment of security analysts by registered securities associations and national securities exchanges	4/15/03

	Original Effective Date
6. Commission Resources and Authority	
601 Authorization of appropriations	7/30/02
602 Appearance and practice before the Commission	7/30/02
603 Federal court authority to impose penny stock bars	7/30/02
604 Qualifications of associated persons of brokers and dealers	7/30/02
7. Studies and Reports	
701 GAO study and report regarding consolidation of public accounting firms	7/30/02
702 Commission study and report regarding credit rating agencies	7/30/02
703 Study and report on violators and violations	7/30/02
704 Study of enforcement actions	7/30/02
705 Study of investment banks	7/30/02
8. Corporate and Criminal Fraud Accountability	
801 Short title	7/30/02
802 Criminal penalties for altering documents	10/31/03
803 Debts nondischargeable If Incurred In violation of securities fraud laws	7/30/02
804 Statute of limitations for securities fraud	7/30/02
805 Review of Federal Sentencing Guidelines for obstruction of justice and extensive criminal fraud	7/30/02
806 Protection for employees of publicly traded companies who provide evidence of fraud	7/30/02
807 Criminal penalties for defrauding shareholders of publicly traded companies	7/30/02
9. White Collar Crime Penalty Enhancements	
901 Short title	7/30/02
902 Attempts and conspiracies to commit criminal fraud offenses	7/30/02
903 Criminal penalties for mail and wire fraud	7/30/02

		Original Effective Date
904	Criminal penalties for violations of the Employee Retirement Income Security Act of 1974.	7/30/02
905	Amendment to sentencing guidelines relating to certain white-collar offenses	7/30/02
906	Corporate responsibility for financial reports	7/30/02
10. Corporate Tax Returns		
1001	Sen se of the Senate regarding the signing of corporate tax returns by chief executive officers	7/30/02
11. Corporate Fraud and Accountability		
1101	Short title	7/30/02
1102	Tampering with a record or otherwise impeding an official proceeding	7/30/02
1103	Temporary freeze authority for the Securities and Exchange Commission	7/30/02
1104	Amendment to the Federal Sentencing Guidelines	7/30/02
1105	Authority of the Commission to prohibit persons from serving as officers or directors	7/30/02
1106	Increased criminal penalties under Securities Exchange Act of 1934	7/30/02
1107	Retaliation against informants	7/30/02

Sarbanes-Oxley Act of 2002
Audit Procedures by Section

102	Is CPA firm registered with PCAOB?	
103	Is CPA firm visiting PCAOB and SEC Web sites for updated information on new audit standards?	
104	Are files reviewed and signed off by partner for PCAOB inspection?	
105	Is CPA firm prepared for any disciplinary action by PCAOB?	
106	Is the CPA firm a foreign firm?	
201	Is the CPA firm independent of bookkeeping, financial information systems, appraisal or valuation, actuarial services, internal audit outsourcing, management functions, human resource services, broker/dealer, investment banking services, investment advisor, legal services, expert services unrelated to the audit, and any other service determined impermissible by PCAOB?	
202	Has the audit committee approved all audit, review, and attest services (in writing)?	
202	Alternatively, has the audit committee pre-approved such according to the issuer's policies and procedures and provided that the audit committee is informed on a timely basis of each service?	
202	If services are pre-approved, do policies ensure that this responsibility is not delegated to management?	
202	For non-audit services, do such services aggregate to 5 percent or less of total revenues paid by the issuer in the fiscal year? (More than 5 percent impairs independence.)	
202	Were non-audit services approved by the audit committee?	

203	The lead audit partner must rotate after 5 years; time out is 5 years, effective for the FIRST fiscal year beginning after 5/6/03. Is the lead partner compliant?	
203	The concurring review audit partner must rotate after 5 years; time out is 5 years, effective for the SECOND fiscal year beginning after 5/6/03.	
	Other audit partners: If they provide 10+ hours of audit service or serve as lead audit partner on a subsidiary for which assets or revenues constitute 20 percent or more of the issuer's consolidated assets or revenues. Is the lead partner compliant?	
204	Prior to filing any SEC filing, has the auditor communicated to the audit committee:	
	1. All critical accounting policies and practices used by the client, including discussions of the reasons why critical accounting estimates or policies are not considered critical, as well as current and anticipated future events impacting these determinations.	
	2. All alternative treatments (accounting and disclosure) of financial information to GAAP have been discussed with the audit committee.	
	3. Other written communication between the auditor and client management, including: schedules of unadjusted differences (i.e., material adjustments and reclassifications), management's representation letter, reports on observations and recommendations on internal controls, engagement letters, and independence letters.	
206	If the auditor is employed by the issuer with a financial reporting oversight role, did this occur one year after the auditor was on the engagement team? (Cutoff = day filing is made with SEC)	

	Have two years of fees been disclosed, including audit fees, audit related fees, tax fees, and all other fees (proxy statements and annual reports)? Effective 12/15/03.	
206	For proxy statements, have the audit committee's pre-approval policies and procedures for audit and non-audit services been disclosed? Have the percentage of auditor's fees where the *de minimis* exception was used by category been disclosed? Effective 12/15/03.	
	The audit partner cannot receive compensation from the audit client, other than from audit, review, or attest services. Is the partner compliant?	
208	Subsections (g) through (l) of Section 10A of the 1934 Exchange Act outline prohibited activity for registered public accounting firms. Is the firm compliant?	
	Are audit committee members independent? If not, national securities exchange can prohibit listing.	
301	Is the audit committee responsible for selecting and overseeing auditor? If not, prohibit.	
	Does the audit committee have procedures for handling complaints regarding accounting practices? If not, prohibit.	
	Is the audit committee authorized to engage advisors? If not, prohibit by exchange.	
	Can the audit committee fund the auditor and any outside advisors? If not, prohibit by exchange.	
302	Quarter and annually, CEO and CFO:	
	1. Must review the financial statements and disclosures being filed.	

302	2. Must ensure the report does not contain any untrue statements or omit any material facts.	
	3. Must ensure financial statements present fairly, materially.	
	4. Are responsible for and have designed, established, and maintained DC&P, and evaluated and reported on the effectiveness of those controls and procedures within 90 days of the report filing date.	
	Is the company compliant? (Consider putting in management letter?)	
	Have all deficiencies and material weaknesses in internal controls been disclosed to the audit committee and auditors?	
	Has fraud, material or not, been disclosed to the audit committee and auditors?	
303	Are the books, records, and accounts falsified?	
304	If there was a restatement, did the CEO and CFO reimburse any incentive bonus received by issuer?	
306	Was there any insider trading (purchasing, selling, or transferring any issuer's equity security during a pension blackout period)?	
401a	Has the issuer provided a separately captioned subsection in MD&A an explanation of off-balance sheet transactions, arrangements, obligations, and other relationships with unconsolidated entities or other persons that could have a material effect? (Effective 6/15/03; annually)	
401a	Has the issuer provided in the MD&A an overview (for registrants other than small business issuers) of certain known aggregate contractual obligations in a tabular format? (Effective 12/15/03; annually)	

401b	Is there disclosure of material information of non-GAAP financial measures (new Regulation G)?	
401b	Amendments to Item 10 of Reg. S-K, Item 10 of Reg. S-B and Form 20-F are made quarterly and annually. Is issuer compliant?	
401b	Has the issuer furnished on Form 8-K public announcements or releases of material nonpublic information regarding results of operations or financial condition (new item 12 of Form 8-K)?	
402	Were any loans made to any director or executive officer?	
403	Were there transactions involving directors, officers, and 10 percent owners? If so, these must be reported within 2 business days (previously 10 business days).	
404	If the issuer is subject to section 13(a) or 15(d) of Securities Exchange Act of 1934, the issuer must have an internal control report:	
	1. Stating the responsibility of management for establishing and maintaining an adequate internal control structure and procedures for financial reporting.	
	2. Containing an assessment of the effectiveness of the internal control structure and procedures of the issuer for financial reporting.	
	3. Requiring the external auditor to attest to assertions made by management in reference to their assessment of internal controls.	
	Companies should have processes to ensure:	
	1. The company's transactions are properly authorized	
	2. The company's assets are safeguarded against unauthorized or improper use.	
	3. The company's transactions are properly recorded and reported.	

406	Does the company have a code of ethics for senior financial officers and contents of that code?	
	If there is a change/waiver of code of ethics, is this reported immediately on Form 8-K?	
	Has the issuer disclosed its code of ethics in their annual reports 10K, 10KSB, 20F, or 40F? (Effective 7/15/03)	
407	The registrant must have an "audit committee financial expert." Therefore:	
	1. Disclose the name and whether independent of management.	
	2. If no expert, disclose the fact and reason.	
	3. Foreign private issuers are included in scope of the final rule with certain exceptions.	
	4. Expert must have knowledge of GAAP.	
	5. Expert must have ability to assess application of principles regarding estimates, accruals, and reserves.	
	6. Expert must have experience preparing, auditing, and analyzing financial statements.	
	7. Expert must have an understanding of internal controls and procedures for financial reporting.	
	8. Expert must have an understanding of audit committee functions.	
	9. Expert must have acquired attributes primarily through experience and education—experience in supervising others, overseeing public accountants, or other relevant experience.	

802	The auditor may not destroy or alter data. Records should be kept for 7 years.	
806	Does the company have whistleblower protection procedures? Establish procedures to report evidence of fraud in a confidential manner and procedures to investigate the matter.	
906	Have the CEO and CFO certified their responsibility for financial reports?	

BIBLICAL DECISION-MAKING CHECKLISTS

Biblical Decision-Making Checklists

This appendix is designed to provide the following groups with tools for decision making that leads to God-honoring behavior and follows the long-term benefits of God's standards as set forth in the Bible. The checklists are not 100 percent of all issues/matters to address; rather they are designed to stimulate the "Tone at the Top" in a manner that the long-term moral consequences of decisions are thoroughly understood and the short-term nature of decisions are not given undue weight.

The following audiences are addressed:

- Board of Directors

- Audit Committees

- Corporate Governance Committees

- CEOs

- CFOs

- Senior Management

- Middle Management

BOARD OF DIRECTORS	
Decision-Making Matters	**Comments**
Establish code of conduct	
Set the "Tone at the Top"	
Selection of a CEO	
Review performance of the CEO	
Selection of board members	
Examine core business models	
Acquisition due diligence	
Merger/acquisition of new entities	
Capital requirements	
Compliance with corporate governance rules and Sarbanes-Oxley Act	
Whistleblower access to board committees	
Listen to independent auditors and legal counsel	
Business performance assessments	
Provide continuing education in corporate governance	
Managing "crisis" issues/situations	

BOARD OF DIRECTORS	
Biblical Principles to Consider	**Comments**
Set the "Tone at the Top" based on principles of honesty and fairness. *"Do things in such a way that everyone can see you are honorable" (Rom. 12:17, NLT).*	
Consider whether the business model and products provide valuable and needed goods and services; seek God's blessing. *"God shall supply all your need according to His riches" (Phil. 4:19).*	
Look to godly standards for the criteria for making decisions (e.g., acquisitions, profitability analysis, setting the "Tone at the Top"). *"Blessed is the man who walks not in the counsel of the ungodly . . . but his delight is in the law of the Lord" (Ps. 1:1–3).*	
Underscore on a regular basis the importance and gravity of the board's position and responsibilities. *"It is a true saying that if someone wants to be an elder, he desires an honorable responsibility" (1 Tim. 3:1, NLT).*	

Board of Directors

Take the time as a group to memorialize in writing the ethical basis for all major decisions, and seek God's help in arriving at a decision that will provide long-term value.

Conclusions/Decisions Made	Ethical Basis/Reasoning

AUDIT COMMITTEE	
Decision-Making Matters	**Comments**
Development of the audit committee charter	
Locating quality members of the audit committee with the required financial and accounting credentials in order to meet the needs of the company within its industry and at its level of complexity	
Identify a qualified financial expert pursuant to the Sarbanes-Oxley Act	
Select an independent accounting firm with the integrity and credentials to perform an examination in accordance with the professional standards	
Work with the CFO to evaluate complex transactions	
Conduct frequent meetings to meet the needs of the agency	
Conduct executive sessions as necessary	
Look to set standards of ethics and integrity over all financial matters	

AUDIT COMMITTEE	
Decision-Making Matters	**Comments**
Seek professionals with extensive experience in GAAP and GAAS training	
Maintain a "continuing education program" to meet the technical accounting/auditing skills needed	
Provide "whistleblower" access	
Be available for the CFO/auditor on an "as-needed" basis	
Provide fraud detection resources	
Comply with Sarbanes-Oxley Act	

AUDIT COMMITTEE	
Biblical Principles to Consider	**Comments**
Build this committee on a strong foundation of: • Technical skills • Desire to stay current on accounting/auditing issues • Appetite for fraud detection • Strong ethics issues *"It is like a person who builds a house on a strong foundation laid upon the underlying rock. When the flood waters rise and break against the house, it stands firm because it is well built"* *(Luke 6:48–49, NLT).*	
Be available for those who have information to make the company's financial statements not misleading. *"Get all the advice and instruction you can, and be wise the rest of your life"* *(Prov. 19:20, NLT).*	

AUDIT COMMITTEE	
Carefully address all material financial issues and transactions in a manner that reflects a thorough review and understanding of the financial position and results of operations of the company and its shareholders who are relying on the audit committee to do its job.	
Conclusions/Decisions Made	**Ethical Basis/Reasoning**

| CORPORATE GOVERNANCE COMMITTEE ||
Decision-Making Matters	Comments
Provide oversight of board responsibilities	
Analysis of board member performance	
Establish continuing education programs for all board members	
Look for balance in board member's independence versus non-independent status	
Coordinate board retreats and special committee meetings	

| CORPORATE GOVERNANCE COMMITTEE ||
Biblical Principles to Consider	Comments
Similar to elders in a church, this committee provides leadership and oversight *"So encourage each other and hold each other up" (1 Thess. 5:11, NLT).* *"The authorities are sent by God to help you" (Rom. 13:4, NLT).*	
This committee must practice the "division of labor" so that the governance burden is shared equitably and properly. *"The godly walk with integrity" (Prov. 20:7, NLT).*	
This committee is the heartbeat of the board, serving with strength and humility. *"The meek shall inherit the earth; and shall delight themselves in the abundance of peace" (Ps. 37:11, KJV).*	

CORPORATE GOVERNANCE COMMITTEE

This committee needs to function in a fluid manner to provide balance and accountability within the board to achieve corporate governance goals and ethics.

Conclusions/Decisions Made	Ethical Basis/Reasoning

CEO	
Decision-Making Matters	**Comments**
Set "Tone at the Top"	
Model "Tone at the Top"	
Hire senior management team	
Lead the senior management team	
Develop business plans and goals	
Oversight of financial systems and controls with CFO	
Provide public commentary on the company's status	
Comply with Section 302 of Sarbanes-Oxley Act	
Emphasize long-term values to shareholders versus short-term greed	
Be concerned about fraud and asset misappropriation	
Care for all employees through "servant leadership"	

CEO	
Biblical Principles to Consider	**Comments**
Ethical leadership is not be underestimated. *"Blessed is the man who trusts in the LORD, whose confidence is in him" (Jer. 17:7, NIV).*	
Biblical guidance is key to great leadership. *"The law of the LORD is perfect, reviving the soul. The statutes of the LORD are trustworthy, making wise the simple" (Ps. 19:7, NIV).*	
Meditate on God's Word for leadership and wisdom. *"Study this Book of the Law continually. Meditate on it day and night" (Josh. 1:8, NLT).*	
Provide a servant leadership "Tone at the Top." *"Whoever wants to be great must become a servant" (Matt. 20:27, THE MESSAGE).*	

CEO	
The CEO must be a "servant leader." Follow the model that Christ set by providing guidance, wisdom, and justice.	
Conclusions/Decisions Made	**Ethical Basis/Reasoning**

CFO	
Decision-Making Matters	**Comments**
Set the "Tone at the Top" regarding financial issues and ethics	
Hire key accounting/financial management, Chief Accounting Officer, and so on	
Thorough understanding of GAAP/ U.S. and International GAAP	
Thorough understanding of good internal accounting control systems	
Maintain high level of fraud detection mechanisms and tools	
Provide financial data for management	
Establish reliable systems to distribute financial data to the public	
Comply with Sarbanes-Oxley Act (e.g., Sections 302/404)	
Raise capital and ensure adequate cash to meet obligations	
Coordinate with audit committee and audit committee chairman	
Maintain continuing education programs for all key accounting personnel	

CFO	
Biblical Principles to Consider	**Comments**
Leadership in financial matters is a challenging but key responsibility for the welfare of all.	
"In all thy ways acknowledge him, and he shall direct thy paths" (Prov. 3:6, KJV).	
CFOs must stand in the gap and hold forth the truth.	
"By standing firm you will gain life" (Luke 21:19, NIV).	

CFO	
The CFO must be a strong individual with concern about cost containment, business ethics, profitability, cash flow, and accountability.	
Conclusions/Decisions Made	**Ethical Basis/Reasoning**

SENIOR/MIDDLE MANAGEMENT	
Decision-Making Matters	**Comments**
Enforcing "Tone at the Top"	
Provide leadership for all employees	
Private and safe work environment	
Be aware of employee difficulties and provide compassion and help as needed	
Enforce internal control systems	
Encourage long-term values vs. short-term greed	
Listen to employees for ideas and reward them for their creativity	
Establish budgets and prepare goals that are reachable	
Provide encouragement	

SENIOR/MIDDLE MANAGEMENT	
Biblical Principles to Consider	**Comments**
Management must echo the "Tone at the Top."	
"Without wise leadership, a nation falls; with many counselors, there is safety" (Prov. 11:14, NLT).	
Being sensitive to the needs of employees and the shareholders of an enterprise is a daily walk in wisdom and discernment.	
"Rejoice with those who rejoice, and weep with those who weep" (Rom. 12:15).	
Look for the gifts that God has given to all employees.	
"I can do everything through him who gives me strength" (Phil. 4:13, NIV).	

SENIOR/MIDDLE MANAGEMENT

Senior and middle management are the "heart and soul" of an organization. They implement policies with attention to details. The application of ethics is critical at this level and enforces the "Tone at the Top."

Conclusion/Decisions Made	Ethical Basis/Reasoning

APPENDIX III

Practical Guide to Compliance with Section 404 of Sarbanes-Oxley Act

COSO OVERVIEW	
Control Environment	
Integrity, ethical values assessment	
Commitment to competence	
Board of directors and audit committee	
Management's philosophy, operating style	
Organizational structure	
Assignment of authority and responsibility	
HR policies and practices	

RISK ASSESSMENT	
Evaluation of objectives	
Operational	
Financial reporting	
Compliance	
Risk identification	
Risk analysis	
Circumstances requiring special attention	
Mechanisms to identify change	

CONTROL ACTIVITIES	
Top-level reviews	
Direct functional or activity management	
Information processing	
Physical controls	
Performance indicators	
Segregation of duties	
Policies and procedures	

INFORMATION AND COMMUNICATION	
Information quality	
Appropriate content	
Timely	
Current	
Accurate	
Accessible	
Communication—Down, across, and up	
Internal	
External	

MONITORING	
• A process that assesses the IC system's performance over time	
• Evaluation process and methodology	
• Reporting deficiencies	
—What	
—To whom	
—Documentation	
—Action plan	

SOX 404 IMPLEMENTATION—PLANNING	
1.	Get audit committee buy-in.
2.	Organize the project.
3.	Develop the project plan.
4.	Get agreement from external auditors on approach and reporting requirements.

GETTING STARTED	
1. Set foundation.	
2. Assess current state of controls.	
3. Identify and document relevant processes.	
4. Evaluate critical processes and controls.	
5. Design and recommend solutions.	
6. Assist in implementation.	
7. Issue report.	

ontracts 1999," introduction by Nell Minow, http://www
hecorporatelibrary.com/ceos/ (accessed October 30, 2003).
Ibid.

Nell Minow, interviewed by Lori Calabro, A CFO Interview, "The Prime of Ms. Nell Minow," *CFO Magazine* 19, no. 5, March 2003, 61.

7. Robert Tie, "The Profession's Roots," *Journal of Accountancy* (November 2003 online issue), http://www.aicpa.org/pubs/ jofa/nov2003/tie.htm (accessed February 19, 2004).

8. Andrew Osterland, "No More Mr. Nice Guy: The State of Finance Audit Firms," *CFO Magazine* 18, no. 9, September 2002, 58.

9. Ibid.

10. Ibid.

11. Kris Frieswick, "How Audits Must Change: Auditors Face More Pressure to Find Fraud," *CFO Magazine* 19, no. 9, July 2003, 48.

12. Ibid.

13. O'Malley, "The Panel on Audit Effectiveness Report and Recommendations," 79.

14. "The Numbers Game," speech delivered by former SEC Chairman Arthur Levitt at the NYU Center for Law and Business, New York, September 28, 1998.

15. William Moran, "Sarbanes-Oxley Opens Doors," *The Practicing CPA* 27, no. 5, October 2003.

16. Frieswick, "How Audits Must Change: Auditors Face More Pressure to Find Fraud," 50.

17. John A. Byrne, "Joe Berardino's Fall From Grace," *Business Week*, August 12, 2002, 51.

18. Daniel Lyons, "Bad Boys," *Forbes*, July 22, 2002.

19. Sec.gov, "Final Rule: Standards Relating to Listed Company Audit Committees," Securities and Exchange Commission, http://www.sec.gov/rules/final/33-8220.htm#P268_78470 (accessed October 31, 2003).

Notes

FOREWORD

1. Boston.com News, Andrew
    Heavy Loads of Corporate Frau
    Archives, http://nl.newsbank.com/ı
    product=BG&p_theme=bg&p_
    maxdocs=200&p_text_search-0=FBI
    %20OR%20cases&s_dispstring=FBI%2
    %20AND%20date(last%20365%20days)&
    0=YMD_date&p_params_date-0=date:B,E&ŗ
    0=-365qzD&p_perpage=10&p_sort=_rank_:.
    ranksort=4&xcal_useweights=yes (accessed Octob
    2003).
2. J. Jameson, (September 30, 2002) One Year Later: The Imp.
    and Aftermath of September 11: "September 11, 2001: Ther.
    and Now" *Online Journal of Issues in Nursing.* Vol. #7 No. #3,
    Manuscript 1. Available: http://www.nursingworld.org/ojin/
    topic19/tpc19_1.htm, (accessed January 28, 2004).

CHAPTER 1 / **Chaos and Confusion**

1. Betsy Atkins, *Corporate Board Member,* November/December
    2003, author's paraphrase.
2. Todd Thomson, interviewed by Tim Reason, A CFO
    Interview, "Citi's New Stance," *CFO Magazine* 19, no. 14,
    November 2003, 80.
3. Shaun F. O'Malley, "The Panel on Audit Effectiveness Report
    and Recommendations," August 31, 2000.
4. Thecorporatelibrary.com, "Company Response Report: CEO

20. Alix Nyberg, "Whistle-Blower Woes," *CFO Magazine,* 19, no. 13, October 2003, 51, 54.

CHAPTER 2 / **"Tone at the Top"**

1. Barbara Ley Toffler, *Final Accounting: Ambition, Greed and the Fall of Arthur Andersen* (New York: Doubleday, 2004).

2. Susan Pulliam, "A Staffer Ordered to Commit Fraud Balked, Then Caved," *Wall Street Journal,* June 23, 2003.

3. Bruce V. Bigelow, "Peregrine," *San Diego Union-Tribune,* March 1, 2003.

4. *San Diego Union-Tribune,* June 17, 2003, 1.

5. *Wall Street Journal,* July 1, 2003, C1.

6. Chick-fil-a.com, "Why We're Closed on Sundays," *Other Features,* http://www.chick-fil-a.com/Closed.asp (accessed October 22, 2003).

7. Chick-fil-a.com, "History," *2000,* http://www.chick-fil-a.com/History.asp (accessed October 22, 2003).

CHAPTER 3 / The Psychology of Fraud

1. Robert Andrews, et al., *The Columbia World of Quotations* (New York: Columbia University Press, 1996), www.bartleby.com/66/ (accessed October 27, 2003).

2. Josh Grossberg, "Sony Fakes a Film Critic," *E! Online News,* http://www.eonline.com/News/Items/pf/0,1527,8370,00.htm (accessed February 26, 2004).

3. Joseph T. Wells, *Occupational Fraud and Abuse* (Austin, TX: Obsidian Publishing Company, 1997), 383–386.

4. Associated Press, "Former CEO Of Aurora Admits Guilt," *Washington Post,* September 5, 2001.

5. Keith Dubay, "Money Manager Gets Five Year in Largest Securities Fraud Investors Deplore Sentence in Scheme That Lost Millions," *Rocky Mountain News,* January 11, 1992, 50.

6. Dan Rafter, "Survey Reports Workplace Fraud, Theft on the Rise," *Chicago Tribune*, October 31, 2000.

CHAPTER 4 / Business Ethics Is a Religious Issue

1. Dr. Kurt Senske, *Executive Values: A Christian Approach to Organizational Leadership* (Minneapolis, MN: Augsburg Books, 2003), 150–151.
2. Ronald Alsop, *Wall Street Journal*, September 17, 2003, R9.
3. *Associated Press State and Local Wire*, August 16, 2002.
4. SmartPros Ltd. 2003, "Ethics Boot Camp Mandatory for Entering MBAs," September 25, 2003, http://accounting.smartpros.com/x40701.xml (accessed January 13, 2004).
5. Stephen Mansfield, *The Faith of George W. Bush* (Lake Mary, FL: Charisma House, 2003), 170–171.
6. Michael S. Heath, *Maine Sunday Telegram*, October 3, 2003, 1.

CHAPTER 5 / Reformation of Corporate America

1. Andrews, et al., *The Columbia World of Quotations.*

CHAPTER 6 / Ancient Foundational Principles for Today's Business Environment

1. Chris Seay, *The Tao of Enron* (Colorado Springs, CO: NavPress, 2002), 12.

CHAPTER 7 / Integrity at Home: Training Future Business Leaders

1. David Paul Tripp, *Age of Opportunity* (New Jersey: P&R Publishers, 2001).
2. Deborah Solomon, "Criminal Convictions of Stewart, Bacanovic Aid SEC's Civil Case," *Wall Street Journal*, March 8, 2004, C1.

3. Andrew Murray, *Raising Your Children to Love God* (Minneapolis: Bethany House, 2001), 119.

4. Glen Schultz, *Kingdom Education* (Nashville, TN: Lifeway Press, 1998), 39.

5. Josh McDowell and Bob Hostetler, *Beyond Belief to Convictions* (Wheaton, IL: Tyndale House Publishers, 2002), 10–11.

6. Barna Research Group, *Third Millennium Teens* (Ventura, CA: The Barna Research Group Ltd., 1999), 48.

7. Andrew Murray, *Raising Your Child to Love God*, 121.

CHAPTER 8 / Responsibility in the Workplace

1. An interview on CBS's *60 Minutes* (aired October 5, 2003), Dr. Sam Waksal, CEO for ImClone Systems Inc.

2. Mark Rutland, *Character Matters* (Lake Mary, FL: Charisma House, 2003), 105.

3. Crosswalk.com, Thayer and Smith, "Greek Lexicon entry for Kurios," *The KJV New Testament Greek Lexicon*. http://www.biblestudytools.net/Lexicons/Greek/grk.cgi?number=2962&version-kjv (accessed October 22, 2003).

4. Todd Hafer, *God's Little Devotional Book for the Workplace* (Tulsa, OK: Honor Books, 2001).

5. James Patterson and Peter Kim, *The Day America Told the Truth: What People Really Believe About Everything That Really Matters* (Upper Saddle River, NJ: Prentice Hall Trade, May 1991).

6. Dwight L. Johnson, *The Transparent Leader* (Eugene, OR: Harvest House Publishers, 2001), 127.

CHAPTER 9 / Following God's Rules: "Beyond Sarbanes-Oxley"

1. Randy Cohen, *New York Times*, December 14, 2003, 76.
2. Editorial, "Corporate Governance: The Road Back," *BusinessWeek*, May 6, 2002, 116.
3. Osterland, "No More Mr. Nice Guy," 50.
4. *Financial Times*, September 24, 15.
5. David Henry and Amy Borrus, Businessweek.com, "Honesty Is a Pricey Policy," Finance, *BusinessWeek Online*, October 27, 2003, http://www.businessweek.com/magazine/content/03_43/b3855136_mz020.htm (accessed October 21, 2003).
6. "Accounting Flaws Spur Exit of the Finance Chief, Key North America Official," *Wall Street Journal*, January 24, 2004, A-9.

CHAPTER 10 / It's All About Character and Integrity

1. Billy Clark, "Court Files Offer an Inside Look at PricewaterhouseCoopers," *Wall Street Journal*, January 5, 2004, 110.
2. *BusinessWeek*, August 12, 2002, 52

Glossary

AICPA: American Institute of Certified Public Accountants

COSO: Committee of Sponsoring Organizations (of the Treadway Commission)

EITF: Emerging Issues Task Force

FASB: Financial Accounting Standards Board

GAAP: Generally Accepted Accounting Principles

GAAS: General Accepted Auditing Standards

PCAOB: Public Company Accounting Oversight Board

SEC: Securities and Exchange Commission

SOX: Sarbanes-Oxley Act

Bibliography

Atkins, Betsy. *Corporate Board Member.* November/December 2003.

AICPA, *The AICPA Audit Committee Toolkit,* 2004.

Barna Research Group, Ltd., 1999, Ventura, California.

Business Week magazine.

CFO Magazine. 2003–2004.

Dubay, Keith. *Rocky Mountain News.* January 11, 1992.

Journal of Accounting. November 2003.

O'Malley, Shaun F., "The Panel on Audit Effectiveness Report and Recommendations." August, 31, 2000.

The Practicing CPA. October 2003.

Mansfield, Stephen. *The Faith of George W. Bush.* Lake Mary, FL: Charisma House, 2003.

McDowell, Josh and Bob Hostetler. *Beyond Belief to Convictions.* Wheaton, IL: Tyndale House Publishers, 2002.

Minow, Nell. The Corporate Library, thecorporatelibrary.com.

Seay, Chris. *The Tao of Enron.* Colorado Springs, CO: NavPress, 2002.

Senske, Kurt, Dr. *Executive Values: A Christian Approach to Organizational Leadership.* Minneapolis, MN: Augsburg Books, 2003.

Wall Street Journal.

Tripp, David Paul. *Age of Opportunity.* New Jersey: P&R Publishers, 2001.

Integrity Advisors Inc.

Integrity Advisors, Inc. is a for profit corporation whose purpose is to advance Bible-based ethics training for:

- Public companies in the U.S.

- . Private companies

- Not-for-profit organizations

- University business schools

- Foreign subsidiaries of U.S. public companies required to report under SOX

It is available for consulting services in a variety of areas that address the COSO requirements to maintain and disseminate morals and ethics training throughout an enterprise. You can contact them at 1-877-4INTGRY (1-877-446-8479) or visit their Web site at www.integrityadvisorsinc.com.